MIDDLE EAST NATIONS IN THE NEWS

Lebanon
IN THE NEWS

PAST, PRESENT, AND FUTURE

David Aretha

MyReportLinks.com Books
an imprint of
 Enslow Publishers, Inc.
Box 398, 40 Industrial Road
Berkeley Heights, NJ 07922
USA

MyReportLinks.com Books, an imprint of Enslow Publishers, Inc. MyReportLinks®
is a registered trademark of Enslow Publishers, Inc.

Library of Congress Cataloging-in-Publication Data

Aretha, David.
  Lebanon in the news : past, present, and future / David Aretha.
      p. cm. — (Middle East nations in the news)
  Includes bibliographical references and index.
  ISBN 1-59845-023-9
  1. Lebanon. I. Title. II. Series.
  DS80,A87 2006
  070.4'4995692—dc22

                                        2005018609

Printed in the United States of America

10 9 8 7 6 5 4 3 2 1

To Our Readers:
Through the purchase of this book, you and your library gain access to the Report Links that specifically
back up this book.
The Publisher will provide access to the Report Links that back up this book and will keep these Report
Links up to date on **www.myreportlinks.com** for five years from the book's first publication date.
We have done our best to make sure all Internet addresses in this book were active and appropriate when
we went to press. However, the author and the Publisher have no control over, and assume no liability
for, the material available on those Internet sites or on other Web sites they may link to.
The usage of the MyReportLinks.com Books Web site is subject to the terms and conditions stated on the
Usage Policy Statement on **www.myreportlinks.com.**
A password may be required to access the Report Links that back up this book. The password is found
on the bottom of page 4 of this book.
Any comments or suggestions can be sent by e-mail to comments@myreportlinks.com or to the address
on the back cover.

Photo Credits: AP/Wide World Photos, pp. 1, 35, 87, 92, 97, 116; BBC Weather, p. 19; Central
Intelligence Agency, pp. 6, 106; City of Beirut, p. 40; © BBC MMV, pp. 11, 20, 44, 67, 99, 100; © CBC
2005, p. 72; © Corel Corporation, pp. 57, 108; © 1996–2005 United Nations, pp. 24, 47; © Rafic Hariri,
Late Prime Minister of Lebanon, 2005, p. 9; © 2005 Cable News Network, p. 95; © 2005 Time, Inc.,
p. 75; © 2000–05 Global Security.org, p. 26; © 2002 ArabNet, p. 48; © 2004 Columbia University Press,
p. 59; © 2004, *The Daily Star*, p. 51; © 2005 WN Network, p. 33; Destination Lebanon, pp. 63, 114; Dick
Doughty/*Saudi Aramco World*/PADIA, p. 29; Discover Lebanon, p. 69; Embassy of Lebanon, pp. 79, 113;
Enslow Publishers, Inc., p. 5; George Baramki Azar/*Saudi Aramco World*/PADIA, pp. 3 (Hariri), 14, 85;
Global IDP Project, p. 91; Library of Congress, pp. 15, 30, 61, 81; MyReportLinks.com Books, p. 4; Nik
Wheeler/*Saudi Aramco World*/PADIA, pp. 3 (Corniche), 77; Photos.com, pp. 7, 38, 43, 53, 55, 65, 105;
The European Commission, p. 111; University of Texas Libraries, pp. 17, 23, 89; U.S. Department of
State, p. 103; Welcome to the Presidential Palace, p. 12; WWF, p. 22.

Cover Photo: AP/Wide World Photos

Cover Description: An SUV burns after the car bombing that killed former Lebanese prime minister
Rafik Hariri. The citizens of Lebanon mourned and protested against the Syrian government, which they
felt was responsible for Prime Minister Hariri's death.

Contents

Family walking along the Corniche

Rafik Hariri

MyReportLinks.com Books
Great Books, Great Links, Great for Research!

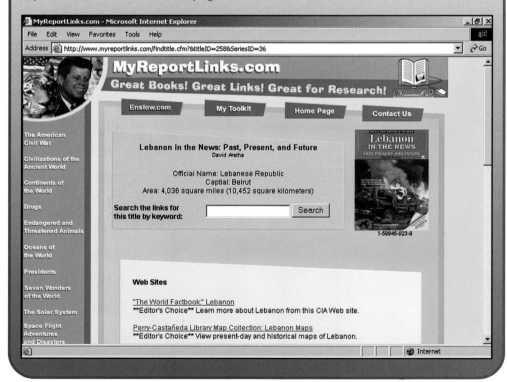

The Internet sites featured in this book can save you hours of research time. These Internet sites—we call them **"Report Links"**—are constantly changing, but we keep them up to date on our Web site.

When you see this "Approved Web Site" logo, you will know that we are directing you to a great Internet site that will help you with your research.

Give it a try! Type http://www.myreportlinks.com into your browser, click on the series title and enter the password, then click on the book title, and scroll down to the Report Links listed for this book.

The Report Links will bring you to great source documents, photographs, and illustrations. MyReportLinks.com Books save you time, feature Report Links that are kept up to date, and make report writing easier than ever! A complete listing of the Report Links can be found on pages 118–119 at the back of the book.

MyReportLinks.com - Microsoft Internet Explorer

File   Edit   View   Favorites   Tools   Help

Address http://www.myreportlinks.com/findtitle.cfm?&titleID=258&SeriesID=36   Go

MyReportLinks.com
Great Books! Great Links! Great for Research!

Enslow.com   My Toolkit   Home Page   Contact Us

The American Civil War
Civilizations of the Ancient World
Continents of the World
Drugs
Endangered and Threatened Animals
Oceans of the World
Presidents
Seven Wonders of the World
The Solar System
Space Flight Adventures and Disasters

Lebanon in the News: Past, Present, and Future
David Aretha

Official Name: Lebanese Republic
Captial: Beirut
Area: 4,036 square miles (10,452 square kilometers)

Search the links for this title by keyword: Search

Lebanon
IN THE NEWS
PAST, PRESENT, AND FUTURE

1-59845-023-9

Web Sites

"The World Factbook:" Lebanon
Editor's Choice Learn more about Lebanon from this CIA Web site.

Perry-Castañeda Library Map Collection: Lebanon Maps
Editor's Choice View present-day and historical maps of Lebanon.

Internet

Please see "To Our Readers" on the copyright page for important information about this book, the MyReportLinks.com Web site, and the Report Links that back up this book.

Please enter **NLE1175** if asked for a password.

Flag
Three horizontal bands: two of red (top and bottom) and one of white (middle). A green cedar tree, the symbol of the country, is centered on the white band.

Official Name
Lebanese Republic

Capital
Beirut

Population
3,826,018 (2005 estimate)

Area
10,452 square kilometers (4,036 square miles)

Highest Point
Qurnat as Sawda at 3,088 meters (10,131 feet)

Lowest Point
Mediterranean Sea at 0 meters

Location
Bordered on the north and east by Syria, on the west by the Mediterranean Sea, and on the south by Israel

Type of Government
Republic

Head of State
President Emile Lahoud

Head of Government
Prime Minister Najib Mikati

Monetary Unit
Lebanese pound

Official Languages
Arabic and French

National Anthem
"All of Us! For the Country, For Our Flag and Glory!"

National Emblem
Cedar tree

Nationality
Lebanese

Religion
Predominantly Islam and Christianity

Life Expectancy
Seventy years

National Holiday
Independence Day (November 22)

1916—*May 6:* During World War I, the Turkish army publicly executes twenty-one Syrians and Lebanese. This event is remembered in both countries as Martyrs' Day.

1920—*April 24:* A condition of the outcome of the San Remo Conference puts Syria and Lebanon under French control. This was part of how the Ottoman Empire was broken up as a condition of its surrender after World. War I.

Baalbek

—*September:* The French work with Lebanese Christians to form the state of Greater Lebanon.

1940—France is occupied by Germany during World War II, and Lebanon falls under the control of the Nazi-led French government known as the Vichy Regime.

1941—Allied soldiers chase the supporters of the Vichy Regime out of Lebanon.

1943—*November 22:* Lebanon becomes an independent country through a League of Nations mandate: France transfers power on January 1, 1944.

1948—The state of Israel is created. Many Palestinians are driven from their former homeland, and many seek shelter in southern Lebanon.

1953—Lebanese women are granted the right to vote.

1967—Israel is victorious in the Six-Day War against Arab nations. As a result, Israel gains more land and more Palestinians flee to Lebanon.

1975—*April:* Four Lebanese Christians are shot dead in a church. The Christian militia called Phalange responds by killing twenty-six Palestinians on a bus. This is the start of the Lebanese civil war.

1976—An Arab League peacekeeping force made up mostly of Syrian troops occupies Lebanon with the support of Lebanese President Elias Sarkis.

1982—June 6: Israel invades Lebanon from the south.

—*September 15:* Israeli troops enter Beirut.

—*September 29:* Israeli troops leave Beirut after a multinational peacekeeping force is deployed.

A city garden

1989—Members of the Lebanese parliament meet in Ta'if, Saudi Arabia, to sign the Ta'if Accord.

2005—*February 14:* Former Lebanese prime minister Rafik Hariri is murdered when a bomb explodes near his motorcade, killing him and fourteen others.

—*April 26:* The last Syrian troops withdraw from Lebanon.

Lebanon in the News

On Valentine's Day, 2005, former Lebanese Prime Minister Rafik Hariri and his motorcade drove along the waterfront in Beirut, Lebanon. A popular billionaire businessman, Hariri had helped restore Lebanon's economy. But he was not

Rafik Hariri is shown here with his wife, Nazik Hariri. He was a popular politician and business leader throughout Lebanon. Learn more about the late prime minister at **Rafic [Rafik] Hariri: The Official Web Site.**

without enemies. Just before one o'clock in the afternoon, a powerful bomb exploded near his motorcade. Hariri and fourteen others were killed, and approximately a hundred people suffered injuries.

To many, Hariri had been a hero—the man who had brought pride and relative prosperity back to the people of Lebanon. All across the country, citizens were outraged by his murder. "I will pick up arms if that is what it takes to bring down the criminals who killed Hariri," said Dina Merhi, a mother of two young children.[1]

An Upset Public

Lebanese citizen Omar Hamade did not believe his people could maintain their cool after the Hariri assassination. "People are leaving unsatisfied and angry," Hamade said after visiting Hariri's burial site. "I am telling you, a cork will burst and all the anger and frustration of the Lebanese people will come in one big explosion and will hit everyone before anything can be done about it."[2]

Since its fifteen-year civil war ended in 1990, the people of the small Middle Eastern country have worked hard to maintain peace. Yet year after year, Lebanon simmers with political conflict and tension. So it goes for a nation that is governed by leaders of multiple religious sects, each with a different agenda. True peace often seems impossible for a nation influenced by neighboring Syria, which the United States and United Nations condemn for harboring terrorists. Conflict is the norm for a country that is fully embroiled in the Palestinian-Israeli crisis. Lebanon, historically part of the "Cradle of Civilization," now lies in the cradle of controversy.

Syria's military occupation may have been the reason for Hariri's assassination. Since 1976 (during Lebanon's civil war), Syria's military forces had occupied Lebanon. In 2005, more than fourteen thousand Syrian troops were still deployed in Lebanon. Their presence was highly controversial. Many Lebanese wanted true

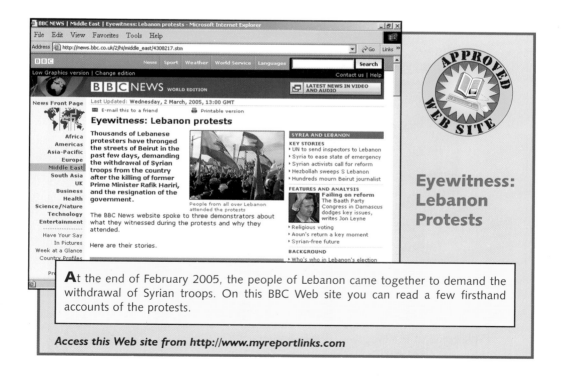

At the end of February 2005, the people of Lebanon came together to demand the withdrawal of Syrian troops. On this BBC Web site you can read a few firsthand accounts of the protests.

Access this Web site from http://www.myreportlinks.com

independence; they wanted to put an end to Syrian occupation. However, Syrian leaders claimed that Lebanon's own armed forces could not maintain order. Lebanon also provided employment to hundreds of thousands of Syrian workers, and their earnings helped bolster Syria's economy.

Lebanese President Emile Lahoud was a strong ally of the Syrian government. He approved of Syria's occupation. However, Hariri publicly opposed Syria's presence. Thus, many speculated

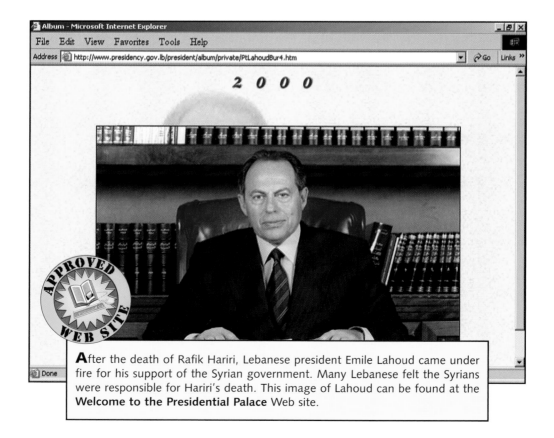

After the death of Rafik Hariri, Lebanese president Emile Lahoud came under fire for his support of the Syrian government. Many Lebanese felt the Syrians were responsible for Hariri's death. This image of Lahoud can be found at the **Welcome to the Presidential Palace** Web site.

that the Syrian government orchestrated the murder to silence their most famous critic.

For the remainder of February, the world did not know for sure if Syria was behind Hariri's murder. However, many anti-Syrian Lebanese demanded that Syria's soldiers leave the country. Of the two hundred thousand Lebanese who gathered for Hariri's funeral, many chanted in Arabic, "Syria out!"[3]

▶ International Pressure

Among those campaigning to kick Syria out of Lebanon was U.S. President George W. Bush. The United States believed that Syria allowed terrorists to live there and build weapons of mass destruction. The United States wanted Lebanon on its side and free of Syrian influence. Said Bush spokesperson Scott McClellan of the Syrians, "[T]hey need to leave Lebanon and let the Lebanese people decide their future."[4]

Feeling the pressure, Syrian leaders agreed to remove all of their troops. On April 26, 2005, in an event that made front pages worldwide, the last Syrian troops left Lebanon.

The problems, however, were hardly over. Though the troops had left, many felt that Syria still had a tight political grip on Lebanon. "Syria controls the presidency, the parliament, and the government and all the other institutions and

Apart from being a billionaire businessman, Rafik Hariri served as prime minister of Lebanon from 1992 to 1998 and again from 2000 to 2004.

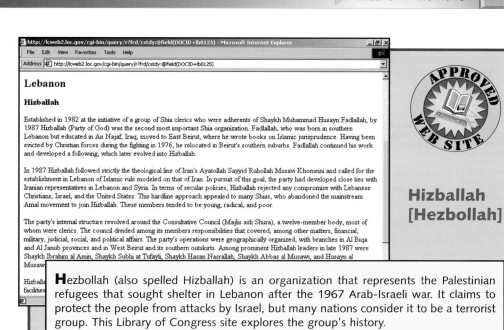

Lebanon

Hizballah

Established in 1982 at the initiative of a group of Shia clerics who were adherents of Shaykh Muhammad Husayn Fadlallah, by 1987 Hizballah (Party of God) was the second most important Shia organization. Fadlallah, who was born in southern Lebanon but educated in An Najaf, Iraq, moved to East Beirut, where he wrote books on Islamic jurisprudence. Having been evicted by Christian forces during the fighting in 1976, he relocated in Beirut's southern suburbs. Fadlallah continued his work and developed a following, which later evolved into Hizballah.

In 1987 Hizballah followed strictly the theological line of Iran's Ayatollah Sayyid Ruhollah Musavi Khomeini and called for the establishment in Lebanon of Islamic rule modeled on that of Iran. In pursuit of this goal, the party had developed close ties with Iranian representatives in Lebanon and Syria. In terms of secular policies, Hizballah rejected any compromise with Lebanese Christians, Israel, and the United States. This hardline approach appealed to many Shias, who abandoned the mainstream Amal movement to join Hizballah. These members tended to be young, radical, and poor.

The party's internal structure revolved around the Consultative Council (Majlis ash Shura), a twelve-member body, most of whom were clerics. The council divided among its members responsibilities that covered, among other matters, financial, military, judicial, social, and political affairs. The party's operations were geographically organized, with branches in Al Biqa and Al Janub provinces and in West Beirut and its southern outskirts. Among prominent Hizballah leaders in late 1987 were Shaykh Ibrahim al Amin, Shaykh Subhi at Tufayli, Shaykh Hasan Nasrallah, Shaykh Abbas al Musawi, and Husayn al Musaw...

Hizballah [Hezbollah]

Hezbollah (also spelled Hizballah) is an organization that represents the Palestinian refugees that sought shelter in Lebanon after the 1967 Arab-Israeli war. It claims to protect the people from attacks by Israel, but many nations consider it to be a terrorist group. This Library of Congress site explores the group's history.

Access this Web site from http://www.myreportlinks.com

political parties," said Amin Gemayel, the former president of Lebanon. Lebanese nationalists will be dissatisfied as long as Syria tries to control their country.[5]

Meanwhile, the militant political party Hezbollah also threatens stability in Lebanon. For years, armed Hezbollah members have clashed with Israeli soldiers along the Israel-Lebanon border, claiming land in the Shebaa Farms area belongs to Lebanon. Many Lebanese support Hezbollah as a defender of their country. Hezbollah also sides with Palestinians in their decades-old conflict against Israel.

United States officials are among those who believe that Hezbollah activities increase tensions in the Middle East. Dr. Robert Rabil, author of *Embattled Neighbors: Syria, Israel, and Lebanon* wrote: "The U.S. is rightly concerned that a conflagration in Shebaa could spread and plunge the whole region into war."[6]

Lebanon cannot handle another major armed conflict. Hamade still grieves for the family members he lost during the horrific civil war. "God," he said upon reflection, "why can't Lebanon find its inner peace?"[7]

Chapter 2 ▶

Land and Climate

It is no wonder that Lebanon attracts throngs of tourists from the Middle East. The country is unique for the region—strikingly beautiful and remarkably diverse. Lebanon is the only Middle Eastern country without desert. In fact, it boasts thick forests and fertile valleys. One can drive from sandy beaches to snow-capped mountains in as little as twenty minutes.

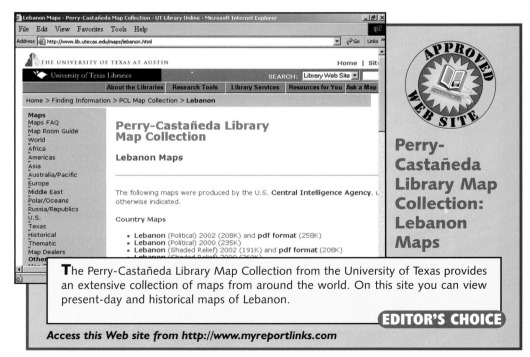

Perry-Castañeda Library Map Collection: Lebanon Maps

The Perry-Castañeda Library Map Collection from the University of Texas provides an extensive collection of maps from around the world. On this site you can view present-day and historical maps of Lebanon.

EDITOR'S CHOICE

Access this Web site from http://www.myreportlinks.com

Lebanon is a tiny country, smaller even than the state of Connecticut. It stretches 135 miles (217 kilometers) from north to south and only 50 miles (81 kilometers) from east to west. The Mediterranean Sea splashes against its entire western border. Lebanon is bordered to the south by Israel and to the north and east by Syria.

The geography of Lebanon can be thought of as four long rows: coast, mountains, valley, and more mountains. Specifically, Lebanon's four geographical regions are the coastal plain, the coastal mountain range (Lebanon Mountains), the central plateau (Bekaa Valley), and the interior mountain range (Anti-Lebanon and Hermon mountains). These regions are so distinct that even their weather is dramatically different.

Coastal Plain

The coastal plain is a strip of land running from north to south, sandwiched between the Mediterranean Sea and the Lebanon Mountains. At no point is it wider than 8 miles (13 kilometers). Some of the beaches are wonderfully sandy, while others are rocky. Various rivers, which empty into the sea, have deposited fertile soil. Even though the coastal plain is the smallest of the country's four regions, it boasts Lebanon's major cities, including the capital Beirut.

Tourists to the coastal region fall in love with the weather. The average daytime temperature in Beirut is 84°F (29°C) in July and 61°F (16°C) in January. Rain rarely falls in the summer, although heavy dews provide enough moisture for vegetation. Winter brings rain and some-times frost, but snow arrives only a few times per century.

The temperature along the coast often is affected by the direction of the wind. West winds (from the sea) cool the area, while east and south winds warm the region. Residents detest the *sharqiyah,* a dry, hot wind from the Indian Ocean that can result in furious sandstorms.

Learn about the weather conditions in Lebanon. This BBC Web site talks about the differences in weather in the low-lying areas and the mountainous regions.

Access this Web site from http://www.myreportlinks.com

Many migratory birds—including pelicans and pink flamingos—thrive in the marshes near the sea. The eastern waters of the Mediterranean Sea lack good nutrients, and therefore have few fish worth catching. Residents in the northern part of the coastal plain, near Tripoli, worry about mosquitoes that carry malaria.

▷ Coastal Mountain Range

The country of Lebanon derives its name from the Lebanon Mountains. Geographers call this area the country's coastal mountain range. Just a few miles from the Mediterranean coast, these mountains are the most prominent physical feature of Lebanon. They stretch approximately 100 miles

The "Country profiles" Web site from the BBC contains information about Lebanon's leaders and media, as well as facts and a basic overview of the country.

EDITOR'S CHOICE

Access this Web site from http://www.myreportlinks.com

(160 kilometers) from north to south and range from 6 to 35 miles (10 to 56 kilometers) east to west.

The highest peak in the Lebanon Mountains is Qurnat as-Sawda. It is more than 10,100 feet (16,000 kilometers) above sea level. The mountains diminish in height the farther south you go. They gradually become the hills of Galilee, just to the south of the Lebanon-Israel border. That is where Jesus lived most of his life.

The Lebanon Mountains have an unusual feature: a layer of nonporous rock that allows water to rise out and form springs. Some of the springs, which are several thousand feet high, flow down the mountains as small rivers. The water helps irrigate land and creates rich soil at high altitudes. In the foothills, farmers have been growing crops for at least four thousand years.

Cedar Trees and Wildlife

Back then, the mountains featured endless forests of cedar trees. Over time, however, most of the cedars were cut down. Now only a few groves of cedars—estimated to be a thousand years old—remain. They are protected as a symbol of the country.

Amid such trees as pines and oaks, wildlife roam the mountains. Deer, squirrels, bears, and wildcats run free in the cedar forests. Eagles, falcons,

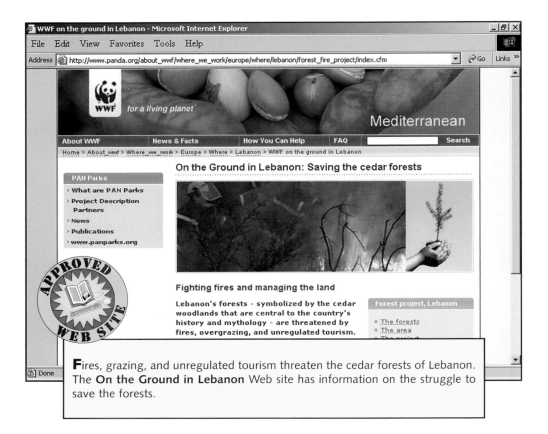

Fires, grazing, and unregulated tourism threaten the cedar forests of Lebanon. The **On the Ground in Lebanon** Web site has information on the struggle to save the forests.

hawks, and woodpeckers fly above. Though the weather is mild in the foothills, it gets cold in the higher regions. During winter, the mountain peaks are blanketed with snow. This attracts many skiers.

▶ Central Plateau

East of the Lebanon Mountains rests the central plateau, known commonly as the Bekaa Valley. This land is so fertile that, in ancient times, it was called the "breadbasket" of the Roman Empire.

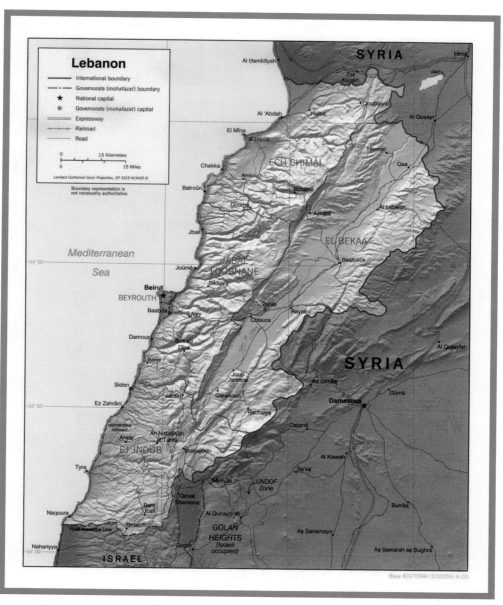

A topographical map of Lebanon showing the location of the mountains and major rivers.

The Bekaa Valley rests on a high plateau between Lebanon's two mountain ranges. Ranging from 6 to 16 miles (10 to 26 kilometers) wide, the valley receives more snow but less rain than the coastal plain. Bekaa Valley's land, however, is wonderfully fertile. Soil and clay deposits, as well as melting snow, flow down from the mountains and hills. As the material washes down, it also brings nutrients that fertilize crops. Moreover, two major rivers—the Litani (flowing south) and the Orontes (flowing north)—provide water for irrigation.

Despite summers that are hot and dry, farmers in the Bekaa Valley produce bountiful crops. They grow everything from wheat and barley to

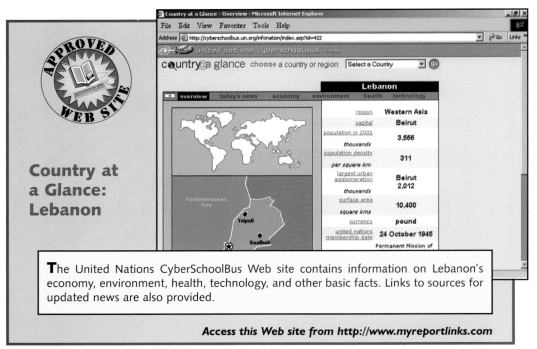

Country at a Glance: Lebanon

The United Nations CyberSchoolBus Web site contains information on Lebanon's economy, environment, health, technology, and other basic facts. Links to sources for updated news are also provided.

Access this Web site from http://www.myreportlinks.com

tomatoes and cucumbers. Goats, sheep, cows, and chickens are among the many farm animals in the valley.

Interior Mountain Range

The interior mountain range, Lebanon's fourth geographical region, runs along the country's eastern border. Standing atop one of its peaks, one can see Lebanon's Bekaa Valley to the west and the country of Syria to the east. The region actually consists of two ranges: the Anti-Lebanon Mountains and the Hermon Mountains. The Barada River separates the two.

These mountain ranges, comprised largely of limestone, are not as rugged as the Lebanon Mountains. However, because of their great height, they accumulate more snow in the winter. Mount Hermon in the south, which rises more than 9,200 feet (2,800 meters) above sea level, is known for its snow-covered peaks.

Centuries ago, the Anti-Lebanon and Hermon mountains were heavily forested. However, deforestation, grazing, plowing, and fires have taken a heavy toll. During World War I, for example, the Turks chopped down huge numbers of trees, using the wood to build railroads. Other occupying countries, including the French and British during World War II, deforested the mountains for fuel or construction. Today, only bushes, bunch grass, and cactuses grow in many areas of the mountains.

Religion

Religion plays a large role in almost every country. But in Lebanon, religion—and religious conflict—has played a huge role in the country's history and politics. In Lebanon, one can only become president or prime minister if he is a certain religion. Civil wars have erupted because religious sects felt they were being neglected

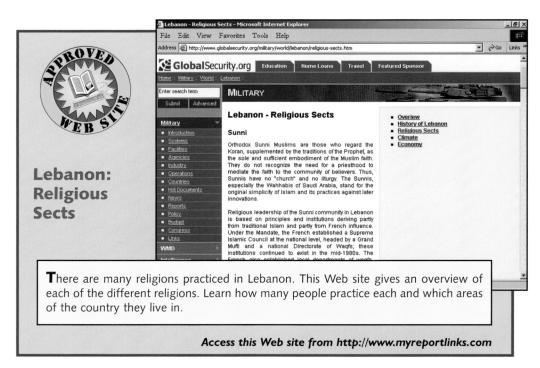

Lebanon: Religious Sects

There are many religions practiced in Lebanon. This Web site gives an overview of each of the different religions. Learn how many people practice each and which areas of the country they live in.

Access this Web site from http://www.myreportlinks.com

politically. In Lebanon, citizens actually have to carry around identification cards indicating whether they are Christian or Muslim.

It is believed that close to 70 percent of Lebanon's population is Muslim and about 30 percent is Christian. However, no one knows the exact figures since the government has not taken a census since 1932. In fact, seventeen religious sects are recognized in Lebanon. Nearly all of the sects are based on Islam or Christianity. The Sunnis, Shi'a, and Druze are the largest Muslim sects.

Lebanese Muslims

All Muslims adhere to the teachings of Muhammad, who started the religion of Islam in the A.D. 600s. Muslims are those who practice Islam. They believe that Allah (Arabic for God) is the only deity and that Muhammad was his messenger. Muslims believe that Jesus was the second to last prophet of God and that Jesus foretold the coming of the last prophet, Muhammad.

About 80 percent of the world's billion-plus Muslims are Sunni. However, the sect comprises only about 20 percent of Lebanon's population. Lebanon's Sunnis, who always have been centered in the country's large coastal cities, are the most orthodox of the Muslim sects. The Sunnis believe that the first four caliphs—Muhammad's successors—rightfully took their place as leaders of the

Muslims. Sunnis have prospered in Lebanon for many hundreds of years. Today, many of them are successful in prominent professions.

Historically, Sunnis felt like they were more a part of the universal Muslim state than they considered themselves to be part of Lebanon. In other words, they aligned themselves more with Sunnis in other areas than with non-Sunnis who also lived in the area that became Lebanon. After Lebanon became independent in 1943, they did not organize well and failed to win appointment or election to important political positions. Today, they are more involved in politics. By law, Lebanon's prime minister must be a Sunni Muslim.

▶ Shi'a Muslims

In the 600s, a sect of Muslims became followers of Ali, the son-in-law of Muhammad. Known as Shi'ites, these Shi'a Muslims grew in power in Egypt and Persia. Eventually they became prominent in Lebanon. Today, Shi'ites account for about 10 to 15 percent of all Muslims worldwide. In Lebanon, they comprise about 35 percent of the country's total population. Averaging five children per family, they are also the fastest growing of Lebanon's major sects.

In modern times, Shi'ites have labored as farmers. They have not been involved in business as much as the Sunnis have. Today, many Shi'ites live as farmers in southern Lebanon and the Bekaa Valley. Some have moved to the poor southern suburbs, known as the "Belt of Misery." Others live in poverty in Beirut.

For years, Lebanese Shi'ites have demanded more political recognition and power. While the speaker of the parliament must be a Shi'ite, that is not a prominent position. Hezbollah, the strongest militant group in Lebanon, is a Shi'a sect. Hezbollah opposes Western nations, such as the United States, and Israel. They would like to

▲ The Mamluk dynasty drove the last of the crusaders out of the Lebanon area in the 1300s. Since then, much of Lebanon has been Muslim. This is a Muslim mosque originally built by the Mamluks in Tripoli, Lebanon.

This photo was taken in 1873 when Lebanon was a part of Syria, a small portion of the Ottoman Empire. The woman in the middle is wearing the garb of a traditional Druze. The other two women are wearing the area's traditional Christian dress of the time period.

see the end of the Israeli state, and consider all of Palestine to be occupied land. Because the United States supports Israel, Hezbollah is at odds with the United States as well. In turn, the United States government considers Hezbollah to be a terrorist organization.

The Druze are the third largest Muslim sect in Lebanon. They are followers of a Shi'ite caliph named al-Hakim, who lived in the eleventh century. The Druze believe that he was God and that he will return.

This sect comprises only about 7 percent of Lebanon's population. The Druze seclude themselves in the mountainous areas southeast of Beirut. A tight-knit group, they remain true to their heritage. The Druze have their own dialect and a distinct style of dress. Secretive in their beliefs, they worship in buildings, not mosques. They are self-sufficient, well organized, and politically successful. The army chief of staff generally has been a Druze.

Lebanese Christians

In the early A.D. 400s, a group of Syrians began to follow the teachings of a hermit named Maron. Considered heretics, Maronites were driven out of Syria by Christians and Arabs. They settled in the Lebanon Mountains. In the 1100s, the Maronites aligned themselves with the Catholic Church.

They were called Eastern Rite Catholics, as opposed to the traditional Roman Catholics.

In the 1600s and 1700s, Maronites migrated to the cities. There they prospered, becoming the most influential sect in Lebanon. As a Catholic people, they fostered a strong relationship with European countries, especially France. When the French took control of the territory after World War I, they bestowed Maronites with more political power than the Muslims.

Maronites in Modern Times

In the early 1900s, Maronites comprised more than half of Lebanon's population. But because of low birth rates and emigration, the Maronites' population in Lebanon is now only about 20 percent. Nevertheless, the law requires that the nation's president must be a Maronite. Moreover, a large percentage of Lebanon's wealthy and well-off population belongs to the sect. The Maronites' power and privilege has caused great resentment by Muslims over the years, leading to violence and war.

In the A.D. 600s, Greek Catholics immigrated to Lebanon. They were known as Melchites. Like the Maronites, they prospered economically, mostly as traders and artisans. Yet Melchites did not concern themselves with politics, and that remains true. Currently, the sect makes up about 15 percent of the Lebanese population, but it is not a political force. The Melchites, comprised of Greek Orthodox and Greek Catholics, speak Greek in some of their church services and traditions. However, they mostly speak Arabic, and they share a feeling of Arab identity.

Armenians are the largest of the remaining sects. Christian immigrants from Turkey, Armenians live mostly in or near Beirut. They, similar to the Maronites, excel in business and various professions.

▶ Religion and Politics

In the United States, law mandates the separation of church and state—religion and government.

The *Lebanon Times* provides current news from Lebanon and the surrounding Middle East nations.

Access this Web site from http://www.myreportlinks.com

But in Lebanon, representation in government is based on religion. By law, the 128-member National Assembly must be represented by sixty-four Christians and sixty-four Muslims. While the country includes secular courts, it also settles matters in religious courts. These special courts handle matters related to specific religions, such as marriage, divorce, and inheritance.

▶ Tolerance

For centuries, religious tolerance has been essential for Lebanon's survival as an independent country. Although, keeping people with such different beliefs happy is a daily struggle. How does a poor Shi'ite accept the fact that the minority Maronites control the presidency? How can a Christian woman not get angry when spousal abuse is deemed acceptable among certain Muslims? Moreover, the memories of civil war still anger Lebanese citizens. Many Muslims living in Lebanon today have had relatives murdered by Christians, and vice versa.

Since the Lebanese civil war, educators have tried to emphasize the importance of tolerance. Lebanon can remain strong only if all sects respect each other. Yet for some Lebanese, other issues are more important than their country's well-being. For example, many Muslims feel a stronger allegiance to the Arab/Muslim world than to their nation. Lebanese Shi'ites, for instance, identify strongly with Iran, a Shi'a-dominated country. Other Lebanese Muslims are sympathetic to the plight of the Palestinians.

In modern times, the Lebanese government has tried to steer clear of its neighbors' conflicts. For example, Lebanon did not participate in the Arab-Israeli wars of 1967 or 1973. It did not participate in the Gulf War in 1991 or the Iraq War that began in 2003. Lebanese have different views on America's ousting of Iraqi dictator Saddam

▲ Thousands of Lebanese celebrate before starting a marathon to mark the thirtieth anniversary of the start of the civil war. The event was held in an effort to strengthen unity among the Lebanese.

Hussein. Many freedom lovers were glad that his oppressive regime was removed, but other Lebanese resented the Western interference.

In Lebanon, religious beliefs affect politics, and political decisions affect religious sects. Turmoil in the Middle East adds to the tension. Thankfully, most Lebanese now realize that some things are more important than politics or religion. For them, tolerance and peace are most precious.

Chapter 4 ▶

Lebanese Culture

Despite their hardships, the Lebanese people are blessed with a rich and diverse culture. Their Arabic heritage, Western influences, and diverse climate create a lively and colorful mix. Only in Lebanon can you find snow skiers and people playing a stringed instrument called an *oud,* women in veils and others in halter tops, all in the same afternoon.

▶ Language

Since Biblical times, Arabic has been the most widely-spoken language of the Middle East. While it is spoken by approximately 200 million people worldwide, the language has dozens of dialects. Even though Lebanon is small, those in different areas of the country speak their own versions of Arabic.

The Arabic language is much different from English. The alphabet has eighteen letters, all consonants. Vowels can be created by adding dashes or dots above or below the words. In school, children learn classical Arabic, which is the country's official language. Elementary schools also teach

▲ *Lebanon is a country full of contrasting lifestyles. Here, a European-style village is nestled next to a large mountain.*

other languages, primarily French and English, which are widely spoken in Lebanon (especially by Christians).

Due to the Armenian genocide by the Turks in 1915–16, a large wave of Armenians migrated to Lebanon. Today, Armenians in Lebanon speak two languages: Armenian in their homes and communities and Arabic elsewhere.

Overall, the Lebanese people can read well. Their literacy rate is more than 90 percent, which is well above the world average.

▶ City Life

Of Lebanon's 3.8 million people, approximately 80 percent live in cities. This makes Lebanon the most urbanized country in the Arab world. More than a million people live in Beirut, the nation's capital.

Once known as the "Paris of the East," Beirut—after sixteen years of civil war—is now called "the city that wouldn't die." Since the war, billions of dollars have been pumped into the reconstruction of Beirut, but with mixed results. Many state-of-the-art apartment and office buildings have been constructed. Yet some of the city's less fortunate still live in bombed-out buildings. Many Beirutis own cars, but the city is choked by traffic congestion and air pollution. Unlike the United States, Lebanon does not have auto emissions standards.

Fumes sometimes form a brownish cloud above the city.

The wealth in Beirut is not evenly distributed. Many are well off, working in such lucrative fields as banking, finance, and advertising. On the other hand, Beirut's once-prominent middle class dwindled during and after the civil war. Many lost their jobs, and thousands of others left the country. Today, a large part of the city's population lives in poverty.

Lebanese law states that children as young as eight can work, and some poor families take advantage of it. Boys work in manual labor, while girls serve as maids for the wealthy. Some children even work on the streets, selling goods.

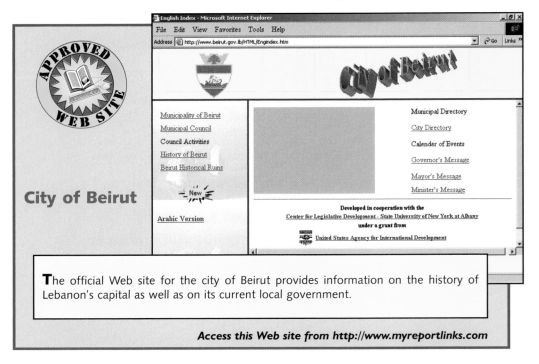

The official Web site for the city of Beirut provides information on the history of Lebanon's capital as well as on its current local government.

Access this Web site from http://www.myreportlinks.com

Beirut does boast numerous attractions, most notably a walkway along the sea called the Corniche. Many residents frequent the cafes that line the Corniche, while others buy fresh corn from vendors and enjoy a pleasant stroll. The city also boasts expensive shops, fancy restaurants, and trendy clubs. Wealthy tourists stay at exclusive resorts. Many of the resort owners, however, have walled off the beaches, denying them to the city's residents.

In recent years, many people—especially Shi'a Muslims—have moved to Beirut's expanding suburbs. Unfortunately, much of the new construction has been built on precious farmland. Moreover, small, wild animals have fled from these areas, causing rodents to run free and multiply.

Tripoli (population 212,000) and Sidon (149,000) are Lebanon's second and third largest cities. Populated largely by Sunni Muslims, the two cities are more conservative and not as westernized as Beirut. They, too, have struggled to rebuild since the war.

Rural Life

Despite the problems that plague Lebanon's big cities, life is even more difficult in the country's rural areas. During the civil war, many rural areas were destroyed or neglected. Ever since the war, many villagers have lived without electricity and running water. Contaminated water has led to the spread of diseases, including hepatitis and dysentery.

Prior to the war, a large percentage of the Lebanese people worked the land, taking advantage of the country's fertile soil. But the effects of the civil war, as well as soil erosion and overuse of pesticides, made farming in many areas impractical or impossible. Many families gave up and moved to the cities. Today, only about 7 percent of the country's workforce is farmers, and most of them are Shi'ites.

Palestinian Refugees and Refugee Camps

The refugee camps in Lebanon are among the saddest places on earth. There are about a dozen refugee camps in the country, spread out from north to south. The largest camp is Ain al-Hilwa, located in the southern city of Sidon. It is home to seventy-five thousand refugees. Of the 350,000 Palestinians in Lebanon, about half live in the camps. Many others live in settlements nearby.

Palestinians are not Lebanese citizens, so they are not entitled to such basic services as schooling. They are banned from dozens of job categories, including such professions as law, engineering, and medicine. Refugees are not allowed to own property, and they are denied access to Lebanon's healthcare system.

▲ Beirut is Lebanon's largest city. After years of civil war, Beirut is slowly prospering once again.

The refugees rely on minimal aid from the United Nations Relief and Works agency. Refugees are extremely poor, and many suffer from malnutrition, disease, and poor dental health. Large numbers of men are permanently disabled due to the war. Children spend their days on the streets with nothing to do amid the stench of garbage and human waste. Mothers agonize over the future of their children.

Amal Akar's daughter painfully suffered from cancer and needed medical treatment. "We borrowed money, and I sent letters to newspapers asking for help—to no avail," Akar said. "I don't mind going anywhere in the world, just get me out

In this online article from the BBC, you can get a glimpse into what life is like for the youth of Lebanon.

Access this Web site from http://www.myreportlinks.com

of here. I don't want to settle in Lebanon. All that we have here is trouble and poverty."[1]

Education

Traditionally, the Lebanese people have placed a strong emphasis on education. Today, young citizens are required to attend at least five years of primary school. Most of them stay in school until age fourteen. At that point, students and their families can choose between academic school (similar to what American children know as high school) or vocational school. More than half of Lebanese children attend private schools because the public schools are poorly funded. Many students drop out of school as teenagers so they can work in the family business or get a job to support the family.

Throughout the Middle East, Lebanon is renowned for its higher education. The prestigious American University of Beirut is one of more than twenty universities in the country.

The Family

In Lebanon, nothing is more important than family. Family members, including grandparents, aunts, uncles, and cousins, tend to live with or near each other. Many work for the family business. Children are expected to uphold the honor of the family, to obey their elders, and do what is in the best interest of the family.

Lebanese fathers are the head of the household and tend to be strict. Yet homes are typically filled with love. Visiting relatives may not come with toys or treats, but they bring enough hugs and kisses for all the children.

Both men and women tend to live at home until they marry. Women usually wed in their twenties, while men typically wait until their thirties. In an effort to maintain the prestige and honor of the family, some parents strongly influence whom their children will marry. However, such arranged marriages are falling out of practice.

▶ Women and Marriage

All marriages, however, must take place in a church. In Lebanon, people rarely marry outside of their religion. When people of different religions do marry, it is almost always a Muslim man marrying a Christian woman, because Islamic law prohibits Muslim women from marrying Christian men. Muslim men are allowed to have more than one wife, although few do.

Women in the cities tend to be better educated than those in rural areas. They also have fewer children and are more likely to enter esteemed professions, including medicine, law, and engineering. Conversely, women in villages devote themselves to the home and family. It is not uncommon for them to bear eight or ten children.

Overall, Lebanese women have more rights than women in other Arab countries. In fact, many have campaigned to eliminate all forms of gender discrimination from the Lebanese constitution. However, laws still reflect old, patriarchal customs. For example, Muslim men have the right to divorce their wives if they do not bear them sons. Moreover, men who commit spousal abuse often go unpunished. And while adultery is illegal for both men and women, the sentences for women are more severe.

▶ The Lebanese "Look"

More than 90 percent of the Lebanese population is Arabic, with less than 10 percent Armenian.

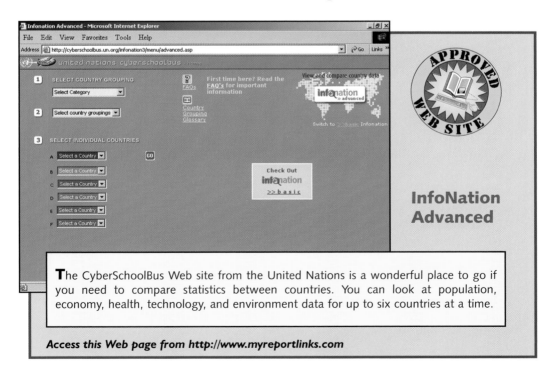

The CyberSchoolBus Web site from the United Nations is a wonderful place to go if you need to compare statistics between countries. You can look at population, economy, health, technology, and environment data for up to six countries at a time.

Access this Web page from http://www.myreportlinks.com

Typically, Lebanese have olive skin with thick, dark hair and big brown eyes. So, too, do Armenians. Some Lebanese, however, have fair skin. A small population has blue or even green eyes.

In Lebanon, people's religion and values are reflected in their dress—especially among women. Christian women tend to wear westernized garb, including dresses, skirts, shorts, and tops. Most Muslim women, especially those in the cities, wear Western clothes, too. However, conservative Muslim women show little flesh in public. They wear long dresses or cloaks, and they cover their heads with scarves. Some wear a veil over their face, especially those in the Druze community.

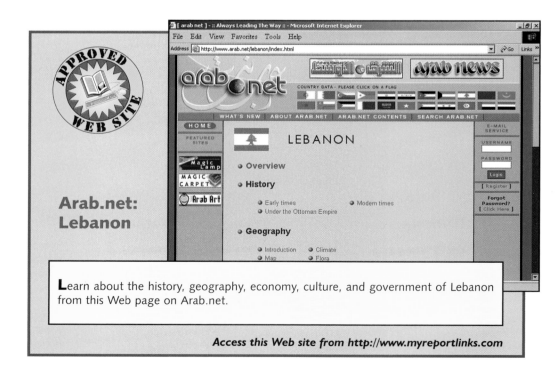

Arab.net: Lebanon

Learn about the history, geography, economy, culture, and government of Lebanon from this Web page on Arab.net.

Access this Web site from http://www.myreportlinks.com

Lebanese men, both Christian and Muslim, have fewer garment restrictions. Like American men, they wear blue jeans, slacks, T-shirts, and business suits. Some Muslim men wear a head scarf called a *kaffiyeh*. The traditional Druze costume for men is quite striking. It includes a long, striped overcoat, baggy pants, and a tall, round hat called a *tarboosh*.

The Arts

In Lebanon, nearly everyone knows the *dabke,* the national folk dance. While in line and holding hands, dancers step and stomp to the beat of a small drum. At every wedding, festival, or large party, people dance the dabke. The Lebanese also enjoy many of the same dances that young people do in American clubs. "Belly dancing," a Middle Eastern tradition in which women in costume shake their bare bellies, is still performed at parties and nightclubs.

The Lebanese enjoy a diverse range of music. Strict Muslims might prefer Arabic folk music, with its lyrical structure and long, sinuous melodies. Arabic classical music, some musicologists believe, is similar to the music of Roman times. Arabic classical is elaborate. It involves an orchestra comprised of musicians playing Western and Eastern instruments.

The oud is the most famous Middle Eastern instrument. While similar to a guitar, its neck is shorter and bent back, and it contains eleven strings. The oud often plays a role in Lebanese fusion music, which combines both traditional and contemporary sounds.

Since the 1980s, many younger Lebanese have embraced pop music, complete with synthesizers and electric guitars. In fact, at the first Arab pop music awards in 2004, Lebanese artists dominated the winners' list. Elissa accepted the award for best music video. Young Lebanese singers Iwan and Carole Samaha won for best male and female newcomers.

Lebanese Movie Industry

Like the country itself, the Lebanese film industry is making a comeback. Prior to the civil war, Lebanon led the Arab world in film production. Lebanese movies were poetic and often explored important topics.

Since the 1990s, many Lebanese films have focused on the war. The internationally acclaimed *West Beirut* (1998) portrays a teenage boy during the first year of the war. A recurring theme in Lebanese films is the protagonist who returns to Lebanon after the war and grapples with the extraordinary changes. Some female directors have interpreted the war through women's eyes.

Filmmakers, however, have to be careful what they portray, as censors will not allow them to taint the government's image. When widely renowned Lebanese director Randa Chahal Sabbag submitted her acclaimed war film *A Civilized People* to censors, they slashed it from 101 minutes to 51. She complained, "There has been a huge national effort to erase and forget all traces of the war."[2]

Lebanon does not have a very large theater community. However, plays in all three Lebanese languages are staged—mostly in Beirut. Some plays are grim commentaries about Lebanon's problems, such as Ziad Rahbani's *Of Dignity and*

The *Daily Star* is Lebanon's leading English-language newspaper. On its Web site, you can read the latest news from Lebanon and the rest of the Middle East.

Access this Web site from http://www.myreportlinks.com

Stubborn Folk. Those who want to escape the harsh realities of everyday life can attend cabaret acts—lavish, feel-good productions.

Traditionally, the Lebanese have been great lovers of literature. Khalil Gibran remains the most famous Lebanese writer of all time. After he dislocated his shoulder as a child in the 1890s, Gibran's family strapped it to a cross and wrapped it for forty days. The Christlike experience added a mystic aura to Gibran, who became a brilliant artist and poet. He wrote romantically about his native Lebanon, and he advocated revolt against Turkish rule. His most famous work is *The Prophet,* a book of twenty-six poetic essays that has since been translated into twenty languages.

▶ Visual Arts

Zajal is a type of poetry unique to the Arab world. A group of poets perform zajal together, often in public competitions. Each poet takes a turn improvising a line. Accompanied by music, food, and chants from the audience, the zajal provides an evening of joyful artistic entertainment.

The artwork of Lebanese painters may reflect either Eastern or Western influences—or often a combination of both. Impressionist Joseph Matar, who has held exhibitions throughout the world, may be the most famous Lebanese artist of all.

Meanwhile, the Basbous brothers are the small country's most renowned sculptors. They turned their village of Rachana, near Tripoli, into a museum of modern art. Their sculptures—made of wood, stone, granite, and metal—line the streets. Michel Basbous even built a house made entirely of found objects. Many tourists of Lebanon cannot wait to visit this enchanting little village.

The Media

During the civil war, numerous militias battled for the hearts and minds of the Lebanese people, and

▲ The cities of Lebanon are highly congested in a lot of places. Here, a small orange grove and garden is surrounded by many large buildings.

they used the media to do it. Together, they ran as many as two hundred radio stations and several dozen television stations. Today, the Lebanese people have far fewer options.

Most of the television stations are privately owned. They broadcast news, talk shows, films, sports, and other entertainment. Much of the programming comes from other countries, both Western and Middle Eastern. News and shows are offered in Arabic, English, and French. As in the United States, music dominates Lebanon's FM radio. The type of music played ranges from Arabic folk music to American rock 'n' roll.

Lebanon has earned high marks for the quality of its newspapers. While the *Beirut Times* and the *Daily Star* are the prominent English-language newspapers, other fine publications are published in Arabic and French. Lebanon's stores offer a variety of magazines, ranging from business to entertainment.

▶ Sports

In the history of the Olympics, Lebanon has never won a gold medal. Its people, however, play a variety of sports with passion and enthusiasm. Almost every community in the country, even small towns and villages, boasts sports programs for young people. Inexpensive ball sports are the most popular kind. Kids all over the country play football (what Americans call soccer), volleyball, and basketball.

Many young boys dream of one day playing in Lebanon's football league, which attracts large crowds in many cities. Horse racing is another popular spectator sport. On Sundays in Beirut, fans place bets on their favorite ponies at the Hippodrome.

Because of the country's varied climate and terrain, Lebanese enjoy numerous outdoor activities. Many jog or Rollerblade along the Corniche, while others hike or bike the mountains. In the

▲ *In Lebanon many people enjoy biking and hiking the mountain trails, or skiing the snow-covered slopes.*

Mediterranean, water lovers swim, sail, water ski, and windsurf. Others kayak down Lebanon's many rivers. Throughout the winter, many take advantage of Lebanon's six ski resorts. The Faraya-Mzaar is the largest resort, offering sixteen ski lifts.

Critics say that hunting and city driving are Lebanon's favorite sports. Few Lebanese own pets (dogs are looked down upon in Arab countries), but many like to hunt. Much of the land is littered with skeletons of hunted animals. On the city streets, air pollution is not the only hazard. Motorists drive as fast as they want—sometimes at a frightening pace—because speed limits and moving violations do not exist. A cautious driver likely will get the horn from an antsy speeder.

▶ Holidays

Because of Lebanon's multiple religious denominations, many holidays fill the calendar. Everyone celebrates New Year's on January 1, with partiers filling the streets and counting down till midnight. National holidays include Independence Day, on November 22, which marks Lebanon's freedom from French rule. Martyrs' Day, on May 6, honors nationalists who were killed by the Turks during World War I.

Muslims adhere to the tenets of Ramadan. As an act of spiritual cleansing, they fast from sunrise to sunset for an entire month. Ramadan is held during the ninth month of the Islamic calendar. Because their calendar is lunar, Ramadan often falls at a different time each year. Muslims break their fast with a great feast called the *Eid al-Fitr.*

Christians celebrate Christmas and Easter, although the Lebanese place greater importance on Easter. In Christian villages, people celebrate a patron saint's day. Each village has a different patron saint, one who offers protection over its people. Maronite Christians look forward to a day of prayer and food on February 9, the Feast of Saint Maron.

▲ *Shish kebab is a favorite dish of the Lebanese and other people living in the Middle East and along the Mediterranean Sea. It can be found at restaurants and barbecues all over the world.*

▶ Lebanese Cuisine

Generally speaking, the Lebanese do not rely on take-out meals, frozen dinners, or other prepared foods from cans or boxes. They make their food themselves. And it is usually fresh, nutritious, and delicious.

Often, the mother or grandmother gets up early to make bread. The bread is as big as a pizza but nearly paper thin. The family will eat bread with their meals throughout the day. It is especially tasty as a wrap for baked *kibbe,* which is a ground meat mixed with wheat, pine nuts, onions, and spices. Many main dishes include meat (often lamb) served with rice, vegetables, spices, and olive oil. Shish kebab, which is skewered vegetables and cubed meat broiled over a fire, is another favorite.

Other healthy delicacies are spinach pies, stuffed grape leaves, hummus (a paste made from chickpeas), and *baba ghannouj* (made from eggplant). All are spiced to please. *Tabbouleh* is a fresh, healthy salad made with tomatoes, onions, wheat, and parsley—with a touch of mint. *Baklava,* which includes layers of flaky pastry, nuts, and syrup, is a classic Lebanese dessert.

Preparing meals and enjoying them together is a great Lebanese tradition and strengthens the all-important family bonds.

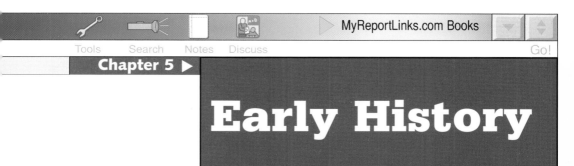
Early History

Historically, Lebanon was the closest thing in the Middle East to Utopia. Its citizens were blessed with fertile land while enjoying the strategic benefit of residing along the Mediterranean Sea. Yet this apparent blessing often became a curse. Numerous empires often sought—and then conquered—this jewel of a territory.

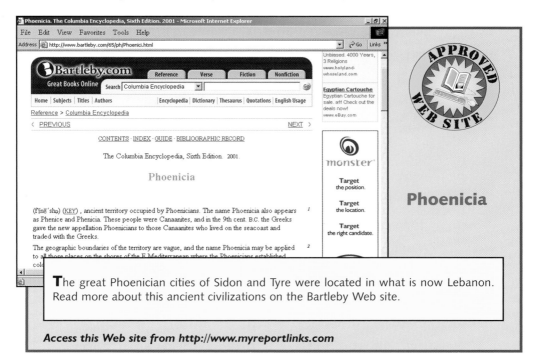

The great Phoenician cities of Sidon and Tyre were located in what is now Lebanon. Read more about this ancient civilizations on the Bartleby Web site.

Access this Web site from http://www.myreportlinks.com

The Phoenicians

Many historians consider Lebanon part of the "Cradle of Civilization." Thousands of years ago, humans in the area raised animals and formed villages. By approximately 3000 B.C., Canaanites established coastal cities in the region. They called their area labnon, due to its snow-capped mountains. Greeks were impressed with the purple *(phoinikies)* dye that the Canaanites sold, and called them "Phoenicians."

Egypt incorporated Phoenicia into its empire from the fifteenth to twelfth centuries B.C. Upon winning their independence, the Phoenicians prospered, achieving extraordinary feats for their times. In about 1200 B.C., the Phoenicians established the world's first alphabet. They produced textiles, worked with metal, carved ivory, and made glass. Moreover, they were renowned for their maritime achievements. They founded colonies along the Mediterranean Sea, such as Cyprus, Rhodes, Crete, and Carthage. They also established trade routes to Europe and western Asia. By 875 B.C., however, the Phoenicians' era of glory ended abruptly.

The Assyrians conquered Phoenicia and remained in power for more than two hundred years. The Phoenician cities of Tyre and Byblos rebelled, but Assyrian rulers crushed the uprisings. In the 600s B.C., the Babylonians seized

This is an image of the columns of the Temple of Jupiter in the town of Baalbeck, the site of the ancient city of Heliopolis.

control of the region. At one point, they enslaved the people of Tyre.

As centuries passed, Phoenicia continued to change hands. The Babylonians gave way to the Persians, who in 346 B.C. killed forty thousand residents of Sidon. In 333 B.C., Persia fell to Alexander the Great, king of Macedonia. In 64 B.C., the Romans added Phoenicia to their extensive empire. After eight hundred years of turmoil, Phoenicia finally entered a long period of peace and prosperity.

While under Roman rule, the people in the Phoenician cities of Byblos, Sidon, and Tyre were granted Roman citizenship. They made pottery and glass, and they exported perfume, jewelry, wine, cedar, and fruit to Rome. The economy boomed. People constructed temples and palaces and even paved roads between cities. Berytus (what is now Beirut) emerged as a prominent city. Even Jesus journeyed to the area, spreading the word of God. Early in the first millennium, Lebanon—like all of the Roman Empire—became Christian.

Enter the Arabs

In A.D. 395, the Roman Empire was divided in two: the eastern (or Byzantine) part with its capital in Constantinople and the western section with its capital in Rome. Lebanon thrived until the sixth

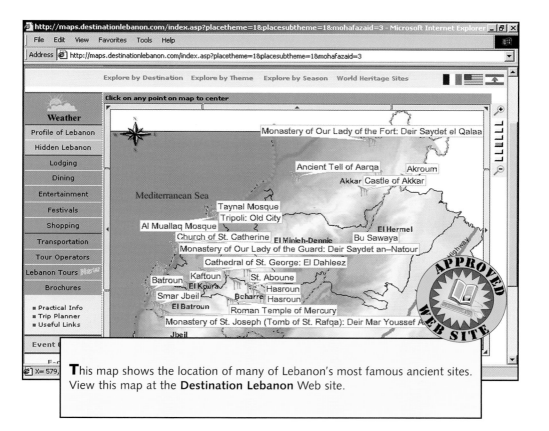

This map shows the location of many of Lebanon's most famous ancient sites. View this map at the **Destination Lebanon** Web site.

century, when earthquakes destroyed Beirut, killing nearly thirty thousand people. By the seventh century, the Roman Empire began to weaken, opening the door for Arab conquest.

The followers of the Prophet Muhammad, the founder of Islam, sought to expand from their base in the Arabian Peninsula. In the 630s, these Muslim Arabs embarked on a jihad, or holy war, against non-Muslims in an effort to convert people to Islam. Beginning in 632, Prophet Muhammad's successor, Caliph Abu Bakr, brought Islam to the area surrounding Lebanon.

An Arab named Muawiyah, the founder of the Umayyad dynasty, was named governor of Syria. That area included present-day Lebanon. Muawiyah established a strong military presence, and in 667 he negotiated a peace agreement with the Byzantine emperor. In 750, the Abbasids, another Arab dynasty, seized power from the Umayyads. The Abbasids ruled Syria and Lebanon until the thirteenth century.

▶ Where They Settled

During the six centuries of Arab rule, an ethnic and religious makeup was established that remains pretty much the same today. Lebanon was home to Byzantine Christians as well as the newly arrived Sunni Muslims, who settled in Lebanon's cities. The region became a refuge for other groups, too. Included was a Christian group called the Maronites, who lived in the Lebanon Mountains.

The Melchites, who were influenced by the Greek Christian theology of Constantinople, also settled in Lebanon. Some of them turned to Catholicism and became known as Greek Catholics. Shi'ite Muslims, followers of Ali (Muhammad's son-in-law), took sanctuary in Lebanon. Finally, a Muslim sect called the Druze

Because Lebanon is part of the "cradle of civilization" many peoples have occupied its land. Thus, there are many historic areas containing ancient ruins.

settled in southern Lebanon. The Druze believed that al-Hakim (996–1021), the Fatimid caliph of Egypt, was an incarnation of God. All of these groups strove for a peaceful coexistence, as they do today. But trouble brewed in the eleventh century when the Christian Crusaders arrived from Europe.

Crusaders

The Crusaders' goal was to win Jerusalem and other places in the Holy Land from the Muslims. Supported by the Byzantine Army, they captured the cities of Tripoli, Beirut, Sidon, and Tyre in the early 1100s. The Crusaders built great castles and churches in Lebanon. They also garnered the support of Maronite Christians—a partnership that angered the region's Muslims. While the Crusaders lost their grip on the region in the 1200s, animosity between Christians and Muslims would remain for centuries.

Mamluks

In the mid-1200s, the Mamluks, from Central Asia, took over Lebanon and the surrounding area. The Mamluks oversaw the region but granted autonomy to the various sects. These included the Maronite Christians, Sunni Muslims, Shi'ite Muslims, and Druze. Up until the 1500s, the cities in the area thrived, intellectually and economically. Beirut became an important trading center between Europe and the Middle East.

Turks

In 1516, the Ottoman Turks invaded Syria. The Turks established a semiautonomous state called Greater Syria. The area included what is now Syria, Lebanon, Israel, and Jordan. With the Ottomans' approval, the Druze rose to become politically dominant in Greater Syria. By the 1700s, however, both the Ottomans and the Druze began to lose their influence. That is when several European countries, most notably France, extended their hands into the region.

▷ European Influence

Ever since the Crusades, the French Catholics had felt akin to the Maronite Christians. In 1648, the French declared themselves protectors of the Christians of Lebanon. In 1770, the area's ruling family, the formerly Muslim Shihabs, converted to Maronite Christianity. The region was becoming more Christian, more French influenced—a situation that the Druze disliked. Their resentment was

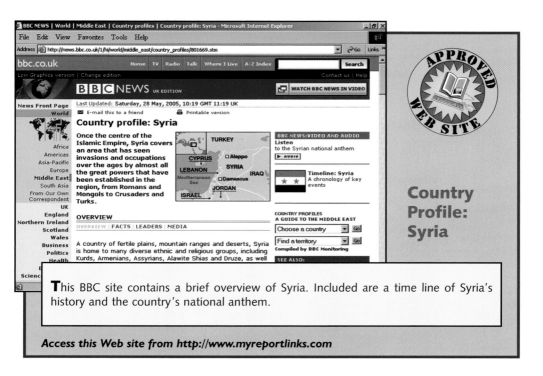

This BBC site contains a brief overview of Syria. Included are a time line of Syria's history and the country's national anthem.

Access this Web site from http://www.myreportlinks.com

inflamed when French Emperor Napoléon tried (unsuccessfully) to conquer Syria. The British, enemies of the French, aligned themselves with the Druze.

Although the Syria/Lebanon region remained part of the Ottoman Empire in the 1800s, the French and British had a heavy influence. Much of it was positive. Some Maronites went to study in Europe and returned to establish schools. British Protestant Christians also started schools in Lebanon. Syria/Lebanon eventually became the most literate province in the Ottoman Empire.

▶ Period of Turmoil

Unfortunately, the region experienced great instability during the 1800s. Bad blood existed between the Maronites and Druze. Bigger trouble arose when Egypt invaded and occupied the region in the 1830s. To expel the Egyptians, Maronites and Druze joined forces. They were supported by more than eight thousand troops from Britain, Turkey, and Austria. Together, they defeated Egypt, but the Druze still were not pleased.

During the Egyptian occupation, the Druze had lost property and power. They resented the Maronites more than ever. Although the Ottoman sultan tried to divide the Lebanon region in two—a northern district for Christians and a southern district for Druze—tensions only increased. From 1845 to 1860, the two sects waged war against one another.

The Druze and Maronites fought over land, power, and religion. The British arrived to help the Druze, and the French supported the Maronites. But the meddling made the situation worse. Wrote historian Kamal Salibi: "Our affairs have become the concern of Britain and France. If one man hits another the incident becomes an Anglo-French affair, and there might even be trouble between the two countries if a cup of coffee gets spilt on the ground."[1]

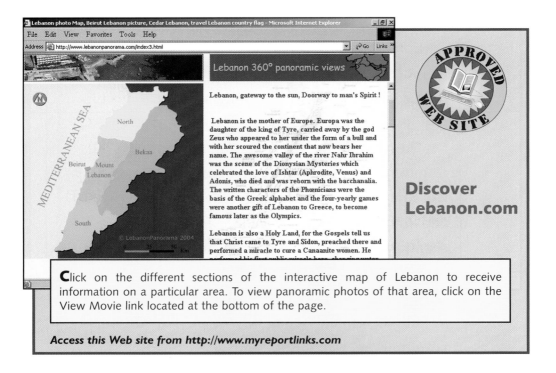

Click on the different sections of the interactive map of Lebanon to receive information on a particular area. To view panoramic photos of that area, click on the View Movie link located at the bottom of the page.

Access this Web site from http://www.myreportlinks.com

Russia also intervened in the war. The Russians supported the Greek Orthodox in their feud with Sunni and Shi'ite Muslims. War in the area of Lebanon peaked in the late 1850s. During one brutal month, Druze attacks left approximately fifteen thousand Christians dead and one hundred thousand homeless.

▶ Restoring Order

Finally, in 1861, European countries worked with the Ottomans to restore order in the region. They established a new government for the area of Mount Lebanon (although it did not include major cities farther away from the mountain, including Beirut, Sidon, and Tripoli). The new government would be led by a *mutasarrif* (governor), a Catholic appointed by the Ottomans. It also included a twelve-member council. Each member represented each of the religious sects in the region.

The new, modern government worked well. A national police force was organized. Roads were built. And new laws detailed citizens' rights and limits. In the late 1800s, Mount Lebanon's economy began to prosper. So, too, did a feeling of nationalism—pride in being Lebanese.

People in the region disliked being governed by the Ottomans. They saw that the Ottoman Empire was crumbling and that other former

Ottoman provinces, such as Greece, were becoming independent. The people of Mount Lebanon also wanted to expand their territory to include Beirut, Sidon, and Tripoli, as well as the Bekaa Valley.

By the turn of the century, citizens of Mount Lebanon had different views about what their nationality was. The Maronites preferred to break away from the Ottomans and the religion Islam, creating a Christian nation. But, of course, Mount Lebanon's Muslims wanted a nation based on their faith and governed by their people. However, these hopes for a new nation gave way to more urgent matters in 1914, when the area of Lebanon became embroiled in World War I.

Back	Forward	Stop	Review	Home	Explore	Favorites	History

Chapter 6 ▶

Modern History

Although most of the fighting during World War I occurred in Europe and Central Asia, the people of Mount Lebanon suffered terribly. The war pitted the Central Powers (Germany, Austria-Hungary, Bulgaria, and the Ottoman Turks) against the Allied Powers (France, Britain, Russia, and the United States). In the area that became

CBC News: Lebanon

The aftermath of a car bombing is seen in Beirut, Lebanon, Feb. 14, 2005. Former prime minister Rafik Hariri was killed in the blast. (AP Photo/Saleh Rifai)

This Web site from the Canadian Broadcast Corporation contains information about Lebanon, as well as a listing of major events in the country's history.

Access this Web site from http://www.myreportlinks.com

Lebanon, the Turks replaced the semiautonomous government with a military occupation.

The Turkish army showed no mercy to the Lebanese people. Led by a harsh Turkish general, Jamal Pasha, they executed hundreds of Christians and Muslims. In early 1915, Jamal established a blockade of the eastern Mediterranean coast to prevent supplies from reaching the Allies. The blockade caused Lebanon to experience horrific famine and plagues. An estimated one hundred thousand people died—one third of the area's population—while others begged for food. Wrote a professor at the American University of Beirut:

> Those who did not flee to the interior in quest of [saving their lives] joined the ever-increasing army of beggars in the city. Among the beggars were those with enough energy to roam the streets and knock at doors, ransack garbage heaps or seek carcasses. Others would lie down on the side of streets with outstretched arms, [starving] bodies and weakening voices. Still others, including infants, could speak only through their eyes.[1]

During the plagues, flies spread typhoid, rats the bubonic plague, and mosquitoes malaria. Contaminated drinking water led to dysentery. In April 1915, swarms of locusts swept overhead.

▶ Martyrs' Day

Moreover, the Turkish army wreaked havoc on Lebanon's forests. They chopped down most of the trees, using the wood to fuel trains or for military purposes. On May 6, 1916, the Turks publicly executed twenty-one Syrians and Lebanese for alleged anti-Turkish activities. To this day, the date is remembered in both countries as Martyrs' Day.

In 1918, Allied forces helped end the misery when they drove out the Turks and occupied Syria and Mount Lebanon. The San Remo Conference was held at the end of World War I, in 1920. At this time the European nations that were part of the Allies formed the League of Nations and divided up the conquered territories. Syria and Mount Lebanon were placed under French control, led by General Henri Gouraud.

State of Greater Lebanon

In September 1920, Lebanon took one step closer to becoming its own nation. The French worked with Lebanese Christians to form the State of Greater Lebanon. As nationalists had sought, the state included the large coastal cities of Beirut, Tyre, Sidon, and Tripoli, as well as the Bekaa Valley. A sectarian form of government was established, with a representative from each religious sect elected to a council.

The state's population was a nearly even mix of Christians and Muslims. However, those who formed the new government determined that the president of Lebanon would always be Christian.

They also ruled that the eleven-member council would include six Christians. To ease resentment by Muslims, the French governor and elected representatives chose a Greek Orthodox—rather than a Maronite Christian—to be the first president.

It did not, however, eliminate the ill will. A 1932 census indicated that Maronites comprised Greater Lebanon's majority, giving them greater representation in government. Muslims, however, insisted the census was rigged. Throughout the decade, Christians and Muslims bickered. Some Christians even formed their own militia, the Phalange. Muslims countered with a militia of their own: the Muslim Scouts. To try to ease

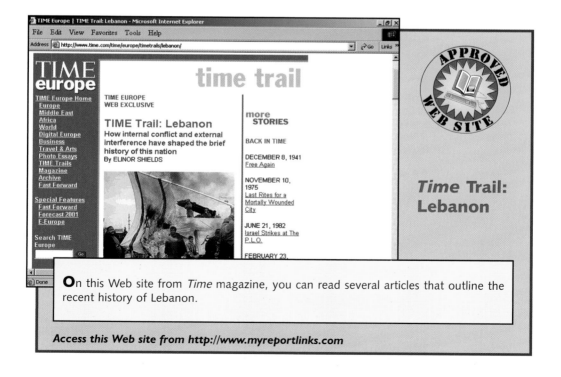

On this Web site from *Time* magazine, you can read several articles that outline the recent history of Lebanon.

Access this Web site from http://www.myreportlinks.com

animosity, the French and Lebanese leaders agreed that Greater Lebanon would become, by 1939, an independent nation. They created a new constitution and elected a Sunni Muslim as prime minister. Plans grounded to a halt, however, with the coming of World War II.

World War II

The Lebanese people finally realized their dream of independence, but it came during a period of extraordinary turbulence. Adolf Hitler's Nazi soldiers occupied France in 1940 and controlled that country until 1944, under what was called the Vichy Regime. The Vichy Regime was in charge of France's colonies, including Lebanon. However, their supporters were ousted from Lebanon in 1941 by British and French resistance fighters.

As soon as they were liberated in 1941, Lebanese leaders declared that Lebanon was independent—free of French influence. They formed a new government, which included a president and his cabinet. French officials responded by arresting the president and cabinet members and suspending the constitution. In November 1943, France—urged by its allies and neighboring Arab countries—released the Lebanese leaders. On November 22, a League of Nations mandate declared Lebanon independent. On January 1, 1944, France handed over the government to

▲ A family takes a relaxing stroll along the Corniche in Beirut, Lebanon. In between World War II and the Lebanese civil war in 1975, Beirut was known as the "Paris of the East."

what is officially known as the Lebanese Republic. At the conclusion of the war, Lebanon joined the United Nations and the League of Arab States. A year later, France withdrew its military forces.

The Golden Years

Led by President Bishara al-Khuri, a Maronite Christian, Lebanon forged ahead in its new era of independence. The nation certainly had obstacles to overcome. The devaluation of the French franc, which was tied to Lebanese currency, hurt the economy. Moreover, because Lebanon refused to join a financial union with Syria, that country imposed sanctions on Lebanon. These factors led to unemployment and a high cost of living in the early postwar years.

Gradually, Lebanon began to prosper. President Khuri worked closely with his premier, a Sunni Muslim. Other Muslims, including Shi'ites and Druze, were appointed to government positions. Government leaders revised press laws and reorganized the judicial system. In 1953, women were granted the right to vote.

Lebanon improved economically, too. With its free-exchange system, it became the banking center of the Middle East. As other Arab nations became rich from oil, more and more money flowed through Lebanon. The country became renowned for its primary educational system, universities, and media. Beirut, the nation's largest city, became known as the "Paris of the Middle East." Besides a bustling economy, the city attracted foreign tourists with its coastal location, dazzling nightlife, and nearby mountain resorts.

Ras Beirut was a hilly peninsula near the American University of Beirut. It became a mecca for artists, poets, writers, and intellectuals. "For nine months of the year," wrote Sandra Mackey in *Lebanon: Death of a Nation,* "life in Ras Beirut was lived in the outdoors. Most people spent hours on their balconies or patios. There they read the

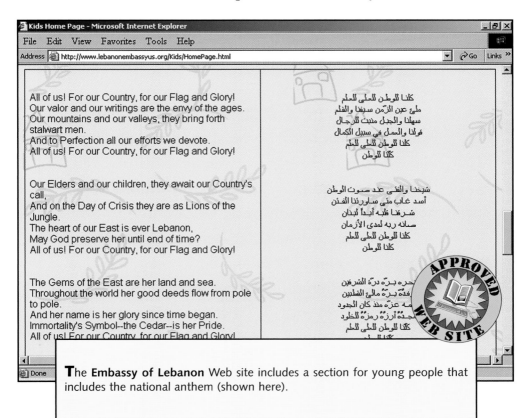

The **Embassy of Lebanon** Web site includes a section for young people that includes the national anthem (shown here).

morning newspapers over Turkish coffee, tended their pot gardens of flowers and herbs . . . or simply sat watching the world go by." At night, Mackey added, the "residents of Ras Beirut whirled through an unending round of parties, receptions, and dances."[2]

The First Postwar Crisis

As in the past, peace and prosperity did not last in Lebanon. A new problem arose in the Middle East in 1948. In the aftermath of the Holocaust, in which the Nazis and their collaborators killed 6 million Jews during World War II, the United Nations established Israel as a nation for Jews. Unfortunately for Arabs, Israel's territory fell on what was previously Palestine, just south of Lebanon. Hundreds of thousands of Palestinians, some Christian but most Muslim, were left home-less. From the moment Israel was formed, Palestinians and their Muslim sympathizers resis-ted the new arrangement.

Approximately 140,000 displaced Palestinians moved north into Lebanon. Many of the Christian Palestinians found jobs and places to live in the country, eventually becoming citizens. The Maronites, however, were troubled by the large number of new Muslims in the country, fearing they would lose political power. Most of the Palestinians settled in refugee camps in southern

Lebanon. There they lived in primitive conditions and without Lebanese citizenship. Though Lebanon's cities thrived during the 1950s, the refugee issue remained troublesome. The Palestinians and Muslim sympathizers within Lebanon believed Palestinians should get their homeland back.

All the while, Lebanese Muslims opposed their country's allegiance to Western countries—namely France, Great Britain, and the United States. Each of these countries was a friend of Israel. In 1956, France, Britain, and Israel warred with Egypt, a Muslim country, over control of the Suez Canal. When Lebanon's leaders refused to break off

▲ A U.S. Marine on patrol in July 1958. Five thousand Marines were sent to restore order in a time of unrest.

relations with France and Britain, many Lebanese Muslims became furious. Instead of maintaining Western ties, Lebanese Muslims wanted their country to join the United Arab Republic (UAR). At the time, the UAR consisted of Egypt and Syria.

In 1957 and 1958, anti-Western sentiment ran high in Lebanon. Muslims assassinated Christian leaders and bombed buildings. They even destroyed the United States' information centers in Beirut and Tripoli. Several thousand people were killed in what was becoming a civil war. Lebanese President Camille Chamoun, fearing his government would be overthrown, asked his Western allies for military support. The United States responded by sending five thousand Marines to help maintain order. The violence finally dissipated when Lebanese General Fouad Chehab was elected president. Chehab made concessions to Lebanese Muslims in an attempt to heal the wounds of the civil war. True peace, though, was still a dream.

Tensions Escalate

As the 1960s progressed, skirmishes between Israel and the Palestinians escalated. In 1967, these skirmishes erupted in the Six-Day War, in which victorious Israel gained control of more land in the region. This caused even more Palestinians to flee. Many went into Lebanon seeking refuge.

Most Lebanese did not want to get involved in the Israeli-Palestinian feud, but it was hard to avoid it. Palestinian fighters based in Lebanon launched raids against Israel. The Israelis typically retaliated. In 1968 they destroyed thirteen planes at the Beirut airport. In May 1969, Israel attacked Palestinian forces in southern Lebanon and occupied territory there for two days.

Muslims within Lebanon sided with the Palestinians, who by 1973 comprised 10 percent of the Lebanese people. The militant Palestine Liberation Organization (PLO) even set up bases in Lebanon. All the while, the surrounding Arab countries, which were united in their hatred of Israel, did not like that Lebanon remained a neutral country.

▶ Upset About Joblessness

Due to a poor economy in the 1970s, many rural Lebanese moved to Beirut. However, few could find decent jobs, and slum areas—which lacked proper sewerage—swelled around the city. At the same time, PLO members became rude and ruthless guests. They took over Lebanese buildings, stole cars, and raped and murdered at will. Many Christians, tired of sharing power with Muslims and sick of the Palestinian crisis, formed militias. Known as the Lebanese Front, these militias included the Phalange and the South Lebanese Army.

Muslims responded with their own militias, which comprised the Lebanese National Movement. They included the PLO, Hezbollah (formed by Shi'a Muslims), Murabitoon (Sunni Muslims), and the Progressive Socialist Party (Druze). These groups supported the Palestinians and wanted greater representation in the Lebanese government. Meanwhile, the weak Lebanese Army splintered, with some members siding with Christians and others siding with the Muslims. The stage was set for yet another civil war.

▶ Civil War Begins

In April 1975, four Lebanese Christians were shot dead in a church. Phalange militiamen responded by killing twenty-six Palestinians on a bus. Days later, PLO members stopped traffic on a busy street and—in front of hundreds of witnesses—exploded a Christian with dynamite. This incident ignited a period of chaos that reigned in Lebanon for many years.

A new government was formed and a cease-fire declared, but it did not matter. The country was up for grabs. Israel blockaded the ports of Sidon and Tyre and invaded southern Lebanon. Some Lebanese, encouraged by the countries of Iraq and Libya, supported the PLO. Muslims gained the upper hand in their war with Christians. Syria, which had supported the

▲ The ravages of the civil war can still be seen in Beirut. In the foreground are sunbathers enjoying themselves poolside at the Summerland hotel, but in the background is the shell of a bombed-out building.

Muslims, switched allegiance to the Christians. They feared that a Muslim victory would trigger Israeli aggression. With Syria's military on its side, Christians became the stronger force.

▶ A Divided Beirut

Much of the fighting took place in heavily populated Beirut. The city was divided by the Green Line, with Christian fighters to the north and Muslims, Druze, and Palestinian militias to the south. Both sides were danger zones. Beirut's port area and hotel district were destroyed. Militiamen killed not just armed enemies but civilians, too. Some people were kidnapped and killed as a form of terrorism.

On December 5, 1975, Phalangists set up roadblocks on city streets. They seized an estimated 350 Muslims and murdered them, in what became known as "Black Saturday." Both sides were consumed with hatred. On January 18, 1976, Christians massacred up to a thousand civilians in Karantina. Two days later, Muslims (many Palestinians) murdered several hundred Christians in Ad Damur.

In November 1976, newly elected President Elias Sarkis directed a thirty-thousand-member Arab League peacekeeping force (mostly Syrians) to take control of the country. The large military presence was successful in keeping the peace, essentially ending the 1975–1976 civil war. But, of course, tensions still simmered.

Chaos Reigns

Beginning in 1976, Syrian peacekeeping troops occupied Lebanon. Bad blood existed between Christians and Muslims during this period, but the feud between the PLO and Israel was the most serious situation. On July 17, 1981, Israel bombed the PLO headquarters in Beirut. The PLO answered with attacks of its own. In June 1982,

A man carries his wounded friend out of the Mayflower Hotel after a rocket struck the building on June 28, 1976.

Israel invaded Lebanon with an enormous force of sixty thousand troops.

In what they called "Operation Peace in Galilee," Israelis pursued the PLO throughout Lebanon. They bombed Tyre and Sidon. For weeks on end, they shelled PLO targets in Beirut. Reckless in their pursuit, Israelis killed an estimated 67,000 people in Beirut, 80 percent of them civilians.[3] Most of the Palestinian fighters fled the country, although some moved to bases in the Bekaa Valley.

The fighting, though, was far from over. On September 14, 1982, Lebanon's Christian president-elect, Bashir Gemayel, was assassinated. Nine days later, Christian militiamen responded by massacring hundreds of Palestinians, including women and children.

In February 1983, the United States, France, Italy, and Britain sent in troops to quell the violence. But their presence provoked more violence. Shi'ite Muslims bombed the U.S. Embassy (killing 63) and the U.S. Marine base (killing more than 240 Americans). Though it boasted the mightiest military in the world, the United States withdrew its troops in 1984.

Escalating Violence

As the 1980s progressed, the situation became even more chaotic. Besides Christians fighting

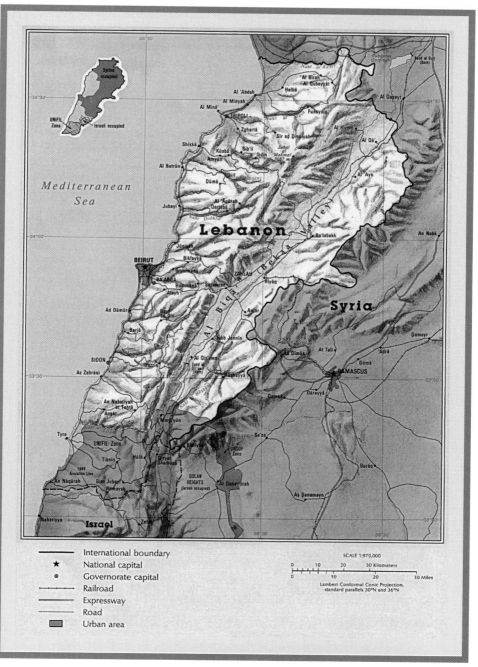

Mediterranean
Sea

Lebanon

Syria

BEIRUT

SIDON

Israel

▲ This map shows the sections of Lebanon that were occupied by Syrian and Israeli forces.

Muslims, many others were involved, including Syria, Israel, the Palestinians, and the United Nations. Moreover, some Lebanese Christian militias fought other Christian militias, and some Muslim groups battled other Muslim groups. In addition, with the army and police unable to keep control, criminal activity rose dramatically. "The society has been destroyed," summarized a Maronite monk. "There is nothing in Lebanon. We are playing in our blood."[4]

The civil war took a heavy toll on civilians. Many thousands were forced to leave their homes, settling in abandoned buildings or shantytowns. Many areas were left without electricity and water. Fearful of being kidnapped, raped, or killed, many citizens rarely ventured outside. Some people relied on Valium, an addictive drug, to help ease their anxiety. For children born in the 1970s, war was all they knew.

▶ Peace at Last

Israel began to withdraw its troops in the mid-1980s, but violence continued. The Amal militias, a military organization of Shi'ite Muslims, so dreaded Israeli attacks that they tried to quell the group that provoked them—the Palestinians. The Shi'ites attacked the Palestinian camps, killing thousands of people. Eventually, occupying Syrian forces were able to end the attacks.

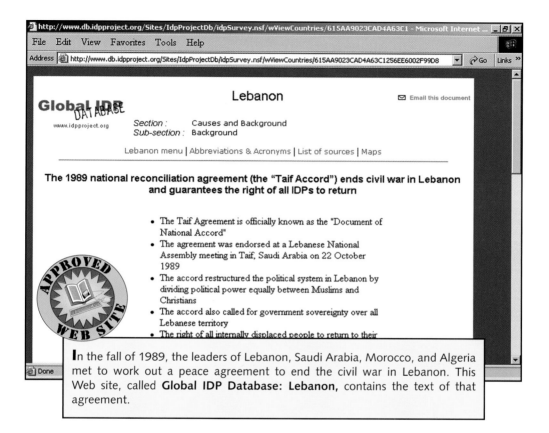

http://www.db.idpproject.org/Sites/IdpProjectDb/idpSurvey.nsf/wViewCountries/615AA9023CAD4A63C1 - Microsoft Internet ...

File   Edit   View   Favorites   Tools   Help

Address   http://www.db.idpproject.org/Sites/IdpProjectDb/idpSurvey.nsf/wViewCountries/615AA9023CAD4A63C1256EE6002F99D8   Go   Links »

Global IDP
DATABASE
www.idpproject.org

Lebanon

✉ Email this document

Section :   Causes and Background
Sub-section : Background

Lebanon menu | Abbreviations & Acronyms | List of sources | Maps

The 1989 national reconciliation agreement (the "Taif Accord") ends civil war in Lebanon and guarantees the right of all IDPs to return

- The Taif Agreement is officially known as the "Document of National Accord"
- The agreement was endorsed at a Lebanese National Assembly meeting in Taif, Saudi Arabia on 22 October 1989
- The accord restructured the political system in Lebanon by dividing political power equally between Muslims and Christians
- The accord also called for government sovereignty over all Lebanese territory
- The right of all internally displaced people to return to their

Done

In the fall of 1989, the leaders of Lebanon, Saudi Arabia, Morocco, and Algeria met to work out a peace agreement to end the civil war in Lebanon. This Web site, called **Global IDP Database: Lebanon,** contains the text of that agreement.

A breakthrough in the war finally came in fall 1989. The Lebanese National Assembly met with the leaders of Saudi Arabia, Morocco, and Algeria and developed a peace settlement called the Ta'if Accord. Although some Lebanese groups did not support the agreement, most Maronite and Sunni leaders did, and it was ratified on November 5.

The Ta'if Accord included a four-point plan for peace. The points were as follows:

1. Muslims and Christians would share half of the cabinet posts and half of the seats in the National Assembly.

2. Steps would be taken to strengthen Lebanon's armed forces, disband the militias, and eventually withdraw Syrian forces.

3. Israeli troops, supervised by United Nations forces, would withdraw completely from Lebanon.

▲ *Cardinal John J. O'Connor of New York, inspects the site of a fuel depot that exploded at Dora in Christian east Beirut on May 29, 1989. The depot blew up after being struck during the fighting between Christian and Syrian forces.*

4. Lebanon and Syria would remain strong allies, promising to uphold the independence and security of each nation.

The Ta'if Accord did indeed end the war (except for border skirmishes between Israel and Palestinians/Muslims). By 1991, Syrian forces and a larger Lebanese Army forced the armed militias to disband. By 1992, all hostages were released and national elections were held for the first time in twenty years.

The war, however, had devastated much of Lebanon. At least 125,000 people, and perhaps as many as 150,000, died in the war. Half a million people fled the country. Eighty thousand Palestinians moved to refugee camps. Approximately half of the country's population was displaced from their homes.

▶ Rebuilding Begins

Throughout the 1990s, workers began to construct new buildings and rebuild Lebanon's infrastructure (mostly in Beirut). But the process was long, slow, and incomplete. By the mid-1990s, a third of the country's population still lived below the poverty level. Many families lived in unsafe, bombed-out buildings. Thousands were permanently disabled by the war, while many suffered psychologically.

Leaders and citizens were so affected by the war that they became committed to peace.

The government made a year's military service mandatory for all Lebanese. General Ali Harb, head of army education, believed that if Christians and Muslims trained and lived together, they would set aside sectarian differences. "We teach them to be Lebanese first, then Druze, Maronite, Shi'ite, or Sunni," Harb said.[5]

By the mid-1990s, attempts at such unity seemed to be working. "A Muslim sleeps in the next bed in my barracks," said Antoine Sacre, a Christian Maronite. "We share our food. He uses my boot polish. I've learned he's a human being."[6]

Recent Tensions

The 2005 assassination of Rafik Hariri made headlines around the world. However, other violent political incidents occurred before and after. On July 19, 2004, Hezbollah official Ghaleb Awali was assassinated by a car bomb outside his home in Harat Hreik. On September 21, 2004, Lebanese authorities announced that ten alleged terrorists

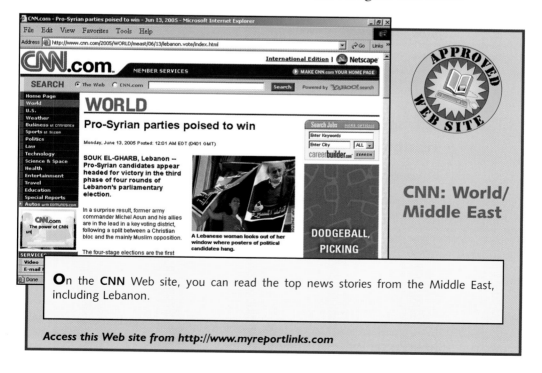

CNN: World/ Middle East

On the **CNN** Web site, you can read the top news stories from the Middle East, including Lebanon.

Access this Web site from http://www.myreportlinks.com

were arrested for plotting to blow up the Italian Embassy in Beirut. And on June 2, 2005, a strong critic of Syria—Samir Kassir of the Lebanese newspaper *An-Nahar*—was killed in a car bombing.

Despite a nationwide effort to achieve tolerance and harmony, political tensions still remain. Bad blood still exists between Lebanese factions and Israel. Those who support Syrian influence in Lebanon are at odds with those who oppose it. Moreover, clusters of terrorists are thought to be hiding throughout Lebanon.

Lebanese psychologist Brigitte Kouri said that political instability in her country jars the nerves of Lebanese citizens. Many still live with the nightmares of the civil war. When the U.S.–Iraq War began in 2003, it worsened tensions in the Middle East. Kouri said that Lebanese citizens experienced "lots of insecurity, lots of anxiety. It's the fear that something could happen here again."[1]

▶ Troubles With Israel

In 2000, Israeli troops finally pulled out of Lebanon. But hostilities around the Israel-Lebanon border have continued ever since. United Nations troops patrol the border, which some call the Blue Line. Israeli soldiers near the line consistently worry about the Palestinians in the refugee camps of Lebanon. Many of the refugees are not only hostile to Israel but well armed.

Meanwhile, Hezbollah, the group credited with driving out Israel in 2000 through timely guerrilla attacks, maintains an armed presence near the Blue Line. Hezbollah claims that the Shebaa Farms area, which is still occupied by Israel, is Lebanese territory. The dispute has caused numerous skirmishes between Hezbollah guerrillas and Israeli soldiers.

Moreover, after Awali's death in July 2004, Hezbollah chief Sheik Hassan Nasrallah admitted that his organization supported the Palestinian cause. As Sarkis Naoum, a commentator for the Lebanese newspaper *An-Nahar*, wrote: "The gravity of the revelation, which was like a kind of admission,

A Hezbollah supporter walks past a tank that was abandoned by the Israelis when they left Lebanon in 2000. Many Lebanese credit Hezbollah with driving Israel out.

is that it confirmed the long-standing Israeli and American accusations that the organization [Hezbollah] 'is involved' in the Palestinian issue and in the Palestinian resistance, arms it, trains it, funds it, and recruits members."[2]

Unlike the Palestinians, who are not considered Lebanese citizens, Hezbollah is officially recognized by the Lebanese government. In fact, a few members of that militant organization comprise Lebanon's 128-member parliament. In the eyes of the United States and the United Nations Security Council, Lebanon, through Hezbollah, has an official link to the Palestinian-Israeli conflict.

The Lebanese government has condoned Hezbollah's activities. However, the UN and United States claim that the group is inflaming tensions between Israel and the Palestinians, which has led to instability throughout the Middle East. Many Lebanese believe that Hezbollah has the right to fight for land that they feel is Lebanon's. However, others worry that the border skirmishes could provoke Israel to launch a major attack on Lebanon, which could spark a major war. That is something that would devastate the fragile country of Lebanon.

▶ The Syrian Occupation

Syria, Lebanon's neighbor to the east, is sixteen times larger than Lebanon. It has more than four

This Web site provides accounts from four Lebanese citizens about their reactions to Syrian withdrawal from their country.

Access this Web site from http://www.myreportlinks.com

times as many people. Also, Syria is an Islamic state and has long considered itself not just a neighbor of Lebanon but a protector of the small country and its Muslim community.

Beginning in 1976, Syrian troops moved into Lebanon during its civil war to help achieve stability. Even when Israel left in 2000, Syrian troops remained. Lebanese President Emile Lahoud supported the strong ties to Syria. However, many leaders within the Lebanese government—from all the major sects—were against the relationship. Walid Jumblatt, leader of the Druze political party, was one of the opponents. "We [the

Lebanese] are mature, we can manage our own affairs, we are clever people," he said.[3]

In 2004, more than fourteen thousand members of the Syrian military still occupied Lebanon. Many Lebanese, especially Christians, clamored for independence. Such demands intensified after the assassination of Hariri, whom many speculated was murdered because of his opposition to Syria's occupation.

Syria did pull out its troops in April 2005. However, it still intended to have a strong hand in Lebanese politics. *An-Nahar* publisher Gebran Tueini even accused Syria of being involved in the murder of his reporter, Kassir: "The Syrians have

BBC News: Middle East

This Web site from the BBC provides all the latest news from the Middle East, including Lebanon.

Access this Web site from http://www.myreportlinks.com

always tried to kill any free voice in Lebanon—any free journalist, any free politician in Lebanon. . . . And what's happening today is a continuation in this regime."[4]

Clearly, Lebanon has a long way to go before it has good relations with its "big brother" neighbor.

Lebanon's Links to Al-Qaeda

Al-Qaeda, which in Arabic means "The Base," is an international terrorist network led by the notorious Osama bin Laden. The network seeks to rid Muslim countries of American and Western influence and to destroy Israel. It is not the only Middle Eastern terrorist group, but it is considered the most dangerous. The organization has orchestrated numerous deadly attacks, including the September 11, 2001, attacks in the United States that killed approximately three thousand people.

Some Lebanese have links to bin Laden's network. Al-Qaeda once was centralized in Afghanistan, but after American forces invaded that country in late 2001, some Lebanese al-Qaeda operatives returned to their home country.

Moreover, other terrorist groups based in Lebanon are allies of al-Qaeda—and potential threats to Western countries. The radical Palestinian group Asbat al-Ansar, which is based in Lebanon, has ties to al-Qaeda. In October 2001, Lebanese forces arrested two Asbat al-Ansar members suspected of planning an attack on the U.S. Embassy in Beirut.

▶ Foiling Al-Qaeda

In September 2004, Lebanese officials made their first arrests of al-Qaeda members. They apprehended twenty al-Qaeda members who were planning to attack Italy's embassy in Beirut. Some were Palestinians, others Lebanese. At the time of their arrest, they possessed 660 pounds (299 kilograms) of explosives. Lebanese Interior Minister Elias Murr said the al-Qaeda members "were also planning to assassinate officials working in western embassies." Murr added that "Lebanon has never seen such a well-organized and dangerous network."[5]

Some believe that al-Qaeda has ties to Hezbollah, the militia that is formally recognized by the Lebanese government. In February 2004, a United States government report stated that "Al-Qaeda also forged alliances with . . . Hezbollah, for the purpose of working together against their perceived common enemies in the West, particularly the United States."[6] However, Lebanese political analyst Haytham Mouzahem stated that al-Qaeda and Hezbollah are "foes rather than friends" due to "very different political priorities, strategies, and agendas."[7]

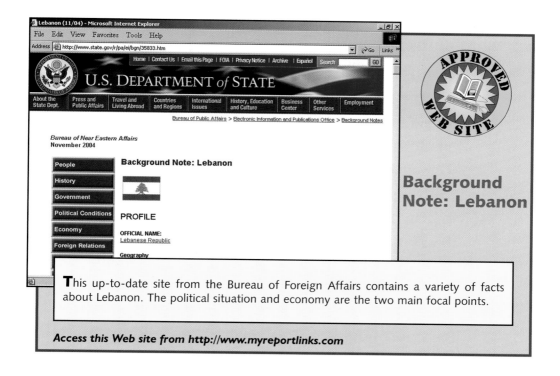

This up-to-date site from the Bureau of Foreign Affairs contains a variety of facts about Lebanon. The political situation and economy are the two main focal points.

Access this Web site from http://www.myreportlinks.com

Nonetheless, the presence of al-Qaeda, Hezbollah, and other terrorist groups in Lebanon has made United States officials very nervous.

▶ Pressure From the United States and United Nations

After the September 11 attacks in 2001, U.S. President George W. Bush tried to build a coalition of nations to fight against terrorism. Bush found Lebanon, with its mix of Western and Middle Eastern influence, to be only somewhat cooperative.

The Lebanese condemned the 9/11 attacks, but they refused United States' demands to freeze Hezbollah's assets. The United States labeled

Hezbollah a terrorist organization, but Lebanon considered Hezbollah's attacks on Israel to be legitimate resistance against a hostile neighbor.

The United States definitely wants Lebanon on its side. It even has given the small nation millions of dollars in aid to woo its support. However, United States officials want their relationship with Lebanon to be on American terms.

On September 2, 2004, the United Nations Security Council—with strong United States influence—passed Resolution 1559. The resolution called for Lebanon's independence to be respected, for Syria's troops to be withdrawn from Lebanon, and for Hezbollah to be disarmed. It also called for the Lebanese government to deploy troops along the Lebanese-Israeli border. A Hezbollah spokesman called the resolution "flagrant interference" in Lebanon's affairs.[8]

Each morning in Lebanon, controversial political figures think twice before starting their cars. Citizens worry daily about more warfare. That, said psychologist Brigitte Kouri, would be unbearable. "I don't think anyone can go through two wars in his lifetime," she said. "One is already plenty."[9]

The Economy

Before his assassination in 2005, former Prime Minister Rafik Hariri helped rebuild a country ravaged by war. The billionaire's company, Solidere, spearheaded reconstruction in Beirut. All across the city, workers constructed new office

▲ From this hillside, the city of Beirut can be seen in the distance. Billions of dollars have been spent in the ongoing effort to rebuild Beirut and other Lebanese cities after fifteen years of civil war.

and residential buildings. New hotels improved Lebanon's image and attracted international tourists.

However, much work still needs to be done. Many of Lebanon's rural areas are in great disrepair. Moreover, because the government borrowed billions of dollars to rebuild, it amassed a huge national debt that it must repay. Thus, the economy is another of the many challenges facing President Lahoud and his government.

▶ Getting by Without Oil

Many Middle Eastern countries flourish because of their lucrative oil wells. Lebanon is not among them. Not only is the nation oil free, but it is also

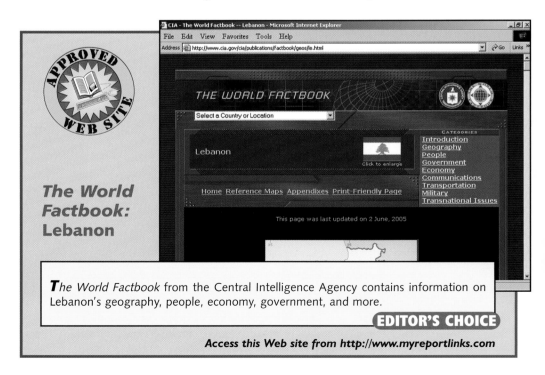

The World Factbook: Lebanon

*T*he World Factbook from the Central Intelligence Agency contains information on Lebanon's geography, people, economy, government, and more.

EDITOR'S CHOICE

Access this Web site from http://www.myreportlinks.com

poor in natural resources. Thus, the Lebanese have had to excel in business and industry in order to thrive as a country. Historically, Lebanon has been a great hub of commerce. Since the 1950s, it has been the banking center of the Arab world.

In Lebanon, the services and banking sectors predominate. They represent 70 percent of the country's gross national product (GNP), which is the total worth of the products and services that the people of a country create. The industrial sector constitutes 20 percent of the GNP, while agriculture accounts for 10 percent.

Banking and Services

The Lebanese government allows as much free trade as possible, with few impediments. This is good news for big business, and it helps make Lebanon a leader in the fields of banking and insurance.

During the oil boom in the 1960s, Lebanon's banks reaped much of the rewards. When countries bought billions of dollars of oil from Arab countries, much of the money flowed through Lebanon's banks. Investments in Lebanon plummeted during the war but bounced back with a vengeance afterward. Total deposits with commercial banks increased from $6.5 billion in 1992 to $33.9 billion in 1999. In 1996, the government reopened the Beirut Stock Exchange.

Dating back to the Phoenicians, Lebanon
has thrived in commerce. Situated along the
Mediterranean Sea, it has handled huge volumes
of imported and exported goods. During the civil
war, the Port of Beirut all but closed down, and
commerce ground to a halt. Since the war, commerce has gradually improved.

Health care and higher education are two
other important service sectors in Lebanon. But
tourism is the business that excites the nation's
planners. With its mild climate and natural
beauty, Lebanon is the oasis of the Middle East.

▲ Tourism and commerce in Lebanon have steadily increased since the end of
the civil war in 1990. This plane is part of the fleet of Trans Mediterranean
Airways (TMA) of Lebanon, which specializes in cargo shipments.

Wealthy foreigners enjoy the resorts by the sea and the hot spots of Beirut. Moreover, Lebanon is the only place to ski in the Arab world.

Prior to the civil war, tourism was responsible for about 20 percent of Lebanon's gross wealth. Since the war's end, as peace has returned and the infrastructure has been improved, tourism has steadily increased. New tourist spots are being built all the time.

Many Lebanese Americans have visited the country in recent years. They either are ex-patriots or descendants of Lebanese emigrants. "This is my roots," said Warren David of Northville, Michigan, who traveled to Lebanon in 2004. "I've got to see it. . . . There are more and more people going back every year."[1]

Construction

From the 1950s until the early 1970s, construction workers erected building after building in Beirut. Eventually, half of the country's population lived in the city. After the war, Beirut experienced a second construction boom. The government and wealthy investors poured billions of dollars into resurrecting the great city. Workers leveled many bombed-out and neglected buildings and erected new ones.

Many citizens complained that the new residential property was unaffordable for most people. It was of no use to the many thousands who lived in poverty. However, the construction boom did create jobs for the many Lebanese men who were unemployed. Construction crews also have worked to rebuild the nation's infrastructure, including roads and telephone service. Much work still needs to be done, though, especially in rural areas. Even in Beirut, no one takes basic services for granted. As late as 2004, Beirutis often were without electricity.

Agriculture

At one time, farming accounted for about 40 percent of Lebanon's economy. But those days are long gone, as the effects of war ruined much of Lebanon's fertile land. Today, about 7 percent of the workforce still toils in agriculture. The nation's most fertile areas are along the coastal strip and in the Bekaa Valley.

Lebanon's diverse topography and climate enable farmers to grow a great variety of crops. Along the coastal plains, they cultivate bananas, citrus fruit, and various vegetables. In the foothills, farmers grow olives, grapes, tobacco, figs, and almonds. And on the mountains' plateaus, farmers produce apples, pears, peaches, plums, cherries, and apricots. During the war, some farmers made a lot of money growing marijuana and opium poppies. But in the early 1990s, those crops were outlawed.

▷ Manufacturing

In 1974, an estimated 130,000 Lebanese people were employed in manufacturing. But during the war, tens of thousands of people lost their jobs. In one dramatic instance, a knitting plant in Beirut that had once employed ten thousand workers was destroyed. Since the war, industry has gradually improved. The government has helped companies prosper by offering tax incentives. Foreign investors, who stayed away from Lebanese companies during the war, now invest heavily.

The EU's Relations With Lebanon

From the official **European Union (EU)** Web site, you can read about the political and economic situations in Lebanon, learn about the country's trade relations with the EU, and more.

Access this Web site from http://www.myreportlinks.com

Today, some of Lebanon's biggest industries are cement, steel, tobacco, textiles, furniture, oil refining, and food processing. Companies also produce detergents, cosmetics, pharmaceuticals, batteries, jewelry, garments, and paper products. Lebanon exports its goods to numerous countries, including Saudi Arabia, Syria, France, and the United States.

On a smaller scale, villagers produce their own specialty items. In small communities across Lebanon, people create pottery, jewelry, baskets, and cutlery. Others excel at embroidery, glass blowing, and woodworking. Though the villagers work primarily for profit, their handiwork adds to the country's culture and charm.

As a result of industry, pollution is an issue in Lebanon. Besides car fumes, the burning of industrial waste pollutes the air. Moreover, raw sewage and oil spills into the coastal waters. Unfortunately, the Lebanese government cannot afford to properly address such environmental issues.

▶ Energy Needs

Lebanon does not possess fossil fuel resources, such as coal and oil, but the country does generate some of its energy. Lebanon is home to three thermal power stations, four gas turbine stations, and seven hydroelectric stations. Oil is imported from neighboring countries. The company

Electricité du Liban (EDL) supplies electricity to the Lebanese people.

Communication and Transportation

When it comes to electronic communications, the Lebanese are fairly well connected. As of the mid- to late 1990s, Lebanon's 3 million-plus citizens owned 330,000 telephones, 120,000 cell phones, 2.85 million radios, and 1.18 million televisions.

A pair of statistics indicate how small Lebanon is compared to the United States. Lebanon has only 4,536 miles (7,300 kilometers) of highway, while the United States boasts 3.9 million miles (6.4 million kilometers). And while Lebanon spends several hundred million dollars per year on

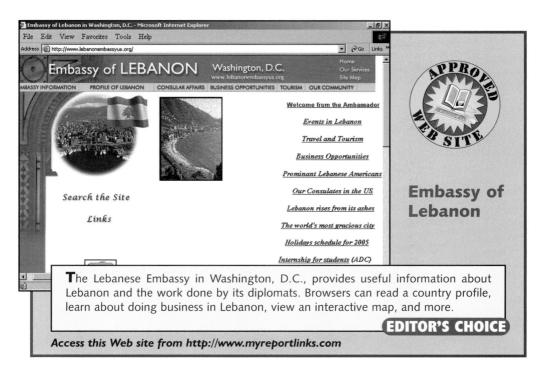

The Lebanese Embassy in Washington, D.C., provides useful information about Lebanon and the work done by its diplomats. Browsers can read a country profile, learn about doing business in Lebanon, view an interactive map, and more.

EDITOR'S CHOICE

Access this Web site from http://www.myreportlinks.com

its military, the United States spends a few hundred *billion* dollars.

Looking Ahead

In most countries, economists fret about the future. In Lebanon, they often panic. After the construction boom in the 1990s, the country's productivity leveled off in the early 2000s. As of 1997, Lebanon's unemployment rate stood at 18 percent—triple that of the United States. As of 1999, a troubling 28 percent of the population lived in poverty.

Explore Lebanon In Summer - Microsoft Internet Explorer

File   Edit   View   Favorites   Tools   Help

Address   http://www.destinationlebanon.com/summer.asp

Explore by Destination   Explore by Theme   Explore by Season   World Heritage Sites

Explore Lebanon in Summer

Weather
Ministry of Tourism
Profile of Lebanon
Hidden Lebanon
Lodging
Dining
Entertainment
Festivals
Shopping
Transportation
Tour Operators

Summer (June-September) in Lebanon is made for sun worshiping, beaches, mountain escapes, and cultural festivals. The clear skies and warm temperatures along the coast, 20-32°C (68-90°F), lure Lebanese and tourists alike to the waters of the Mediterranean. The atmosphere here is a mixture of trendy "see and be seen" and utter relaxation.

As usual, Lebanon offers tourists more than a traditional "sun and fun" vacation. When not soaking up the sun, visitors can soak up some history at a plethora of <u>archeological sites</u>. For a change of pace, head to the mountains. Plenty of outdoor activities, including <u>hiking</u>, <u>rafting</u>, and <u>mountain biking</u> await in the cooler mountain climes, 6-22°C (45-70°F).

For music, dance, theatre, and other arts enthusiasts, summer is when Lebanon hosts a large number of summer festivals, featuring local and international performers. The largest of these festivals are held at historic and archaeological sites, serving as breathtaking backdrops for performances. For example, the <u>Baalbeck Festival</u> is hosted on the site of spectacular Roman temples; the <u>Beiteddine Festival</u> is held at a 200 year-old palace in the mountains of the Shouf; and the <u>Byblos Festival</u> takes place in one of the oldest continuously inhabited cities in the world.

These festivals attract premier talent in a variety of performance areas, ranging from opera or jazz to renowned dance companies and famous comedians. Some notables throughout the years have included stars such as Gilberto Gil, Sting, the Paris Opera Ballet, Nigel Kennedy, and Jose Carreras.
For festivals on a smaller scale with more of a local flavor, many cities and towns throughout the country host summer fairs or festivals.

The **Destination Lebanon** Web site describes the cultural events and tourist attractions that are found in Lebanon during different times of the year.

Moreover, Lebanon is burdened by a huge national debt. The government owes billions of dollars to other countries. A large percentage of citizens' tax money is spent on the interest for those loans.

In recent years, Lebanon was encouraged by its tourism industry. The country was the destination of one million visitors in 2003, and in 2004, that number reached an exciting 1.4 million. However, after the assassination of former Prime Minister Rafik Hariri in February 2005, leaders worry about the state of the economy. "Tourism and instability cannot live together," said Lebanese hotel owner Pierre Achkar.[2]

In Need of Stability

Even worse, many feel that the stability of the nation itself is in jeopardy. The Hariri assassination plunged Lebanon into its worst political crisis since the civil war. Said citizen Dina Merhi after Hariri's murder, "I am willing to spread blood to release the hate I feel in my heart. After Hariri's death, I fear nothing. If civil war in Lebanon or war against Syria is the answer, so be it."[3]

Others, however, believe that the people of Lebanon will not allow another civil war to occur. "The sectarianism of the past doesn't exist," said citizen Majd Houmani. "Just go visit Hariri's grave and you will see how Lebanese are united."[4]

▲ Lebanese children pray at the grave site of former prime minister Rafik Hariri.

Indeed, lining the graves of Hariri and his companions were pictures of the Virgin Mary, verses from the Qu'ran, and a poster that featured a brown cross (a Christian symbol) with a yellow Islamic crescent. "I just hope this unity lasts," said Houmani, "and Hariri's death will forever be the symbol of sectarian peace in Lebanon."[5]

Nearly all of Lebanon's citizens, especially those who recall the horrors of war, share the same hope.

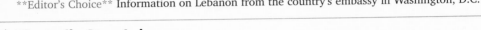

The Internet sites described below can be accessed at http://www.myreportlinks.com

▶**The World Factbook: Lebanon**
Editor's Choice Learn more about Lebanon from this CIA Web site.

▶**Perry-Castañeda Library Map Collection: Lebanon Maps**
Editor's Choice View present-day and historical maps of Lebanon.

▶**Young in the Arab World: Lebanon**
Editor's Choice A look into the life of Lebanese youth.

▶**Embassy of Lebanon**
Editor's Choice Information on Lebanon from the country's embassy in Washington, D.C.

▶**The Daily Star: Lebanon**
Editor's Choice Read daily news from Lebanon and the Middle East.

▶**Country Profile: Lebanon**
Editor's Choice Examine a profile of this Middle Eastern country.

▶**Arab.net: Lebanon**
This Web site provides general information on Lebanon.

▶**Background Note: Lebanon**
Travelers to Lebanon should check out this site from the U.S. State Department.

▶**BBC News: Middle East**
Get the latest news from the Middle East.

▶**CBC News: Lebanon**
An overview of the country of Lebanon.

▶**City of Beirut**
Welcome to the capital of Lebanon.

▶**CNN: World/Middle East**
Read the latest news from Lebanon and the Middle East.

▶**Country at a Glance: Lebanon**
Information on Lebanon from the United Nations.

▶**Country Guide: Lebanon**
The BBC has information on the weather in Lebanon.

▶**Country Profile: Syria**
Learn about Lebanon's neighbor, Syria.

Report Links

The Internet sites described below can be accessed at
http://www.myreportlinks.com

▶**Destination Lebanon**
What to do and see in Lebanon.

▶**DiscoverLebanon.com**
View panoramic photos from around Lebanon.

▶**The EU's Relations with Lebanon**
Learn about Lebanon's relationship with the European Union.

▶**Eyewitness: Lebanon Protests**
The Lebanese people protest against the Syrian occupation.

▶**Global IDP Database: Lebanon**
An agreement brings the civil war in Lebanon to an end.

▶**Hizbollah [Hezbollah]**
This site gives information on the organization known as Hezbollah.

▶**InfoNation Advanced**
The United Nations provides a number of statistics for the countries of the world.

▶**Lebanon: Religious Sects**
Learn about the religions of Lebanon and how they effect relations.

▶*Lebanon Times*
Read an English-language daily newspaper from Lebanon.

▶**On the Ground in Lebanon: Saving the Cedar Forests**
Learn about environmental issues in Lebanon.

▶**Phoenicia**
Read this encyclopedia entry about the Phoenician civilization.

▶**Rafic [Rafik] Hariri: The Official Web Site**
Read about the former prime minister of Lebanon.

▶**Syria Withdrawal: Lebanese speak**
Read the reactions from the Lebanese people after the last of the Syrian troops left the country.

▶*TIME* **Trail: Lebanon**
A look into the recent history of Lebanon from *Time* magazine.

▶**Welcome to the Presidential Palace**
The official Web site of current Lebanese President Emile Lahoud.

al-Qaeda—An international terrorist network led by Osama bin Laden.

Blue Line—The Israel-Lebanon border, which has been contested by both sides. It is patrolled by United Nations troops.

dabke—Lebanon's national folk dance.

Druze—Followers of an eleventh-century Shi'ite Muslim caliph named al-Hakim, whom they believe was God.

Green Line—The line that divided Beirut during the Civil War, with Christian militias to the north and Muslims, Druze, and Palestinian fighters to the south.

gross national product—The total worth of the products and services that the people of a country create.

guerrillas—Soldiers who wage a "hidden" war, launching surprise attacks and then retreating.

Hezbollah—A Shi'ite organization committed to the removal of Israeli troops from Lebanon.

Islam—The name of the religion that was initiated by Muhammad early in the seventh century. Islam literally means "surrender to Allah (God)."

kaffiyeh—A head scarf worn by some Muslim men.

kibbe—A Lebanese delicacy made with ground meat, wheat, pine nuts, onions, and spices.

Maronites—Christians who follow the teachings of a fourth-century hermit named Maron.

Melchites—Greek Catholics who immigrated to Lebanon in the 600s.

militia—A fighting force that is not part of the regular army.

nationalism—Loyalty and pride in a nation of similar or like-minded people.

oud—A Middle Eastern instrument similar to a guitar, although with eleven strings and a shorter neck.

Palestinians—Those who lived in Palestine and their descendents. Tens of thousands were left homeless after the formation of Israel.

Phalange—A Christian paramilitary organization formed in Lebanon in the 1930s.

Phoenicians—A prosperous people who inhabited the area that is now Lebanon beginning in 1200 B.C.

PLO—The Palestine Liberation Organization, founded in 1964. It is dedicated to regaining land for Palestinians that currently is controlled by Israel.

Ramadan—A holy month of fasting for Muslims.

sectarian—Relating to, influenced by, or having the qualities of religious sects.

Shi'ites—Muslims who are followers of Ali, the son-in-law of Muhammad.

Sunnis—Members of the branch of Islam that accept that the first four caliphs were rightful successors to Muhammad.

Ta'if Accord—A peace agreement ratified in 1989 that put an end to Lebanon's civil war.

tarboosh—A tall, round hat worn by Druze men.

zajal—Arabic folk poetry involving improvised lines from multiple participants.

Chapter 1. Lebanon in the News

1. Rym Ghazal, "Will tragedy unite or divide us?" *The Daily Star,* February 21, 2005, <http://www.dailystar.com.lb/article.asp?edition_id=1&categ_id=2&article_id=12836> (February 27, 2005).

2. Ibid.

3. Associated Press, "Lebanese ex-PM's family urges killing probe," *MSNBC,* February 17, 2005, <http://www.msnbc.msn.com/id/6967302/> (February 18, 2005).

4. Leena Saidi and David Stout, "Huge Car Bomb Kills Lebanon's Former Prime Minister," *The New York Times,* February 14, 2005, <http://www.nytimes.com/2005/02/14/international/14cnd-beirut.html?ex=1109826000&en=6ffd407b51bd43be&ei=5070&hp> (February 18, 2005).

5. "Lebanese reaction to Syrian pullout," *BBC News,* April 26, 2005, <http://news.bbc.co.uk/1/hi/world/middle_east/4485741.stm> (June 4, 2005).

6. Robert Rabil, "Should We Be Worried About Hezbollah?" *History News Network,* December 23, 2002, <http://hnn.us/articles/1168.html> (June 4, 2005).

7. Rym Ghazal, "Will tragedy unite or divide us?"

Chapter 4. Lebanese Culture

1. Alaa Shahine, "Poverty trap for Palestinian refugees," *The Palestine Monitor,* March 29, 2004, <http://www.palestinemonitor.org/factsheet/poverty_palestinian_refugees.htm> (December 16, 2004).

2. Lee Hockstader, "Lebanon's Forgotten Civil War," *The Washington Post,* December 20, 1999, p. A24.

Chapter 5. Early History

1. Kamal Salibi, *The Modern History of Lebanon* (New York: Caravan Books, 1996), p. 79.

Chapter 6. Modern History

1. Philip K. Hitti, *Lebanon in History: From the Earliest Times to the Present* (London: MacMillan & Co., 1957), p. 485.

2. Sandra Mackey, *Lebanon: Death of a Nation* (New York: Contemporary Books, 1989), p. 9.

3. "Encyclopedia: History of Lebanon," *Nationmaster.com,* n.d., <http://www.nationmaster.com/encyclopedia/History-of-Lebanon> (January 8, 2005).

4. Mackey, *Lebanon: Death of a Nation,* p. 222.

5. Lara Marlowe, "Up from Despair," *Time Europe,* January 15, 1996, <http://www.time.com/time/europe/timetrails/lebanon/leb960115.html> (January 10, 2005).

6. Ibid.

Chapter 7. Recent Tensions

1. Lucy Williamson, "Iraq war stirs anxiety in Lebanon," *BBC News,* October 14, 2003, <http://news.bbc.co.uk/2/hi/middle_east/3183870.stm> (November 19, 2004).

2. Michael Matza, "Israel: Attacks aided from outside," *philly.com,* September 5, 2004, <http://www.philly.com/mld/inquirer/news/nation/9582617.htm> (January 6, 2005).

3. Scott Wilson, "Sectarian Tensions Simmer in Lebanon," *Washington Post,* October 13, 2004, <http://www.lebanonwire.com/0410/04101301WP.asp> (November 26, 2004).

4. "Lebanon strike call after bombing," *CNN.com,* June 3, 2005, <http://edition.cnn.com/2005/WORLD/meast/06/02/beirut.blast> (June 4, 2005).

5. Roman Kupchinsky, "Analysis: Is Al-Qaeda

Operating In Lebanon?" *GlobalSecurity.org,* n.d., <http://www.globalsecurity.org/security/library/news/2004/09/sec-040929-rferl01.htm> (November 19, 2004).

6. Adam Zagorin and Joe Klein, "9/11 Commission Finds Ties Between al-Qaeda and Iran," *Time,* July 16, 2004, <http://www.time.com/time/nation/article/0,8599,664967,00.html> (November 23, 2004).

7. Haytham Mouzahem, "Hizbullah and Al-Qaeda: Friends or foes?" *The Daily Star,* August 20, 2004, <http://www.dailystar.com.lb/article.asp?edition_id=10&categ_id=5&article_id=7532> (November 24, 2004).

8. "Lebanon furious over US envoy's 'interference,'" *Middle East Online,* November 19, 2004, <http://www.middle-east-online.com/english/lebanon/?id=11935> (November 25, 2004).

9. Lucy Williamson, "Iraq war stirs anxiety in Lebanon," *BBC News,* October 14, 2003, <http://news.bbc.co.uk/2/hi/middle_east/3183870.stm> (November 19, 2004).

Chapter 8. The Economy

1. Niraj Warikoo, "Homeland Beckons to Michigan Lebanese," *Detroit Free Press,* November 22, 2004, <http://www.aaiusa.org/news/must_read11_22_04.htm> (February 20, 2005).

2. Steven Komarow, "Bombing Could Thwart Beirut's Turnaround," *USA Today,* February 17, 2005, <http://www.usatoday.com/printedition/money/20050218/a_beirut18.art.htm> (February 20, 2005).

3. Rym Ghazal, "Will tragedy unite or divide us?" *The Daily Star,* February 21, 2005, <http://www.dailystar.com.lb/article.asp?edition_id=1&categ_id=2&article_id=12836> (February 27, 2005).

4. Ibid.

5. Ibid.

Bechara, Soha. *Resistante: My Life for Lebanon.* New York: Soft Skull Press, 2003.

Byers, Ann. *Lebanon's Hezbollah: Inside the World's Most Infamous Terrorist Organizations.* New York: Rosen Publishing Group, 2002.

Conley, Kate A. *Lebanon.* Edina, Minn.: ABDO Publishers, 2004.

Fisk, Robert. *Pity the Nation: Lebanon at War.* New York: Oxford University Press, 2001.

Friedman, Thomas L. *From Beirut to Jerusalem.* New York: Anchor Books, 1990.

Goldstein, Margaret J. *Lebanon in Pictures.* Minneapolis: Lerner Publications, 2004.

Hutchison, Linda. *Lebanon.* San Diego: Greenhaven Press, 2003.

McDaniel, Jan. *Lebanon.* Philadelphia: Mason Crest Publishers, 2004.

Ousseimi, Maria. *Caught in the Crossfire: Growing Up in a War Zone.* New York: Walker and Co., 1995.

Willis, Terri. *Lebanon.* New York: Children's Press, 2004.

Zwicker Kerr, Ann. *Come with Me from Lebanon: An American Family Odyssey.* Syracuse, N.Y.: Syracuse University Press, 1994.